It Happened In

# It Happened In Seattle

## Remarkable Events That Shaped History

## Steve Pomper

Guilford, Connecticut

Project editor: David Legere
Map: Daniel Lloyd © 2010 by Morris Book Publishing, LLC

Library of Congress Cataloging-in-Publication Data is available on file.

ISBN 978-0-7627-4368-1

Printed in the United States of America

10 9 8 7 6 5 4 3 2 1

# CONTENTS

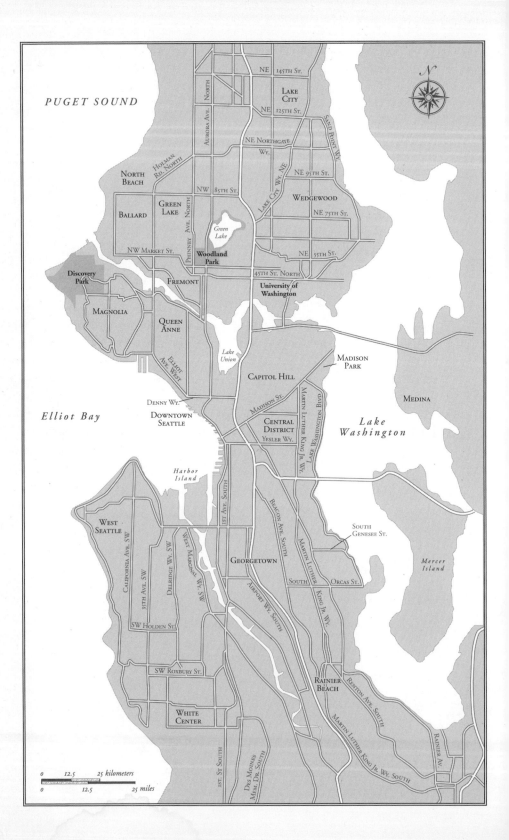

# CONTENTS

# INTRODUCTION

Seattle is unique and almost mystical among large American cities, tucked away as it is in the oft-misty gray shroud of the Great Pacific Northwest. Once you've delved into Seattle's history, something becomes immediately apparent: Arthur Denny and his compatriots chose the perfect spot to plant a city, for not only is it a natural beauty but also a convenience for commerce, which has led Seattle to its remarkable livability compared with many major American cities. Two spectacular mountain ranges, stunning ocean beaches, and expansive high deserts wait only hours from the heart of the Emerald City, not to mention the deep water, protected harbor, which makes Seattle one of the busiest ports in the United States.

Why the correlation between livability and commerce? Well, those aspects were about all that mattered to the founders of this fair city, who felt the two went hand in hand. In fact, Bill Speidel tells us in his immensely readable "biography" of early Seattle, *Sons of the Profits,* "If they [Seattle's founders] could have made more money by *not* building a city, then that is what they would have done." Incidentally, when the settlers founded the first, albeit temporary, pioneer colony at New York-Alki in West Seattle, virtually the first thing they did was to cut down some trees and sell the timber to businessmen with cargo ships bound for San Francisco, inaugurating Seattle's founding industry.

Few American cities can boast the amenities, both natural and man-made, that Seattle can. Some of these we must attribute to nature's providence: magnificent snowcapped mountain ranges, the vast and deep Puget Sound, and the crisp, clean air. Other city features were created by the enterprising hands of Seattle's entrepreneurs: innovative industries, spectacular sports venues, world-famous landmarks like the Space Needle and the Pike Place Market, and restaurants, theaters, and retail shops in abundance. While we can't credit Seattle's founders with creating the natural features, we are indeed fortunate they chose such a location to build their city.

When the Denny Party landed on the wind-whipped, rainy shoreline at Alki Point in today's West Seattle, it immediately set to carving a new home out of the wilderness soon to be called Seattle, a name honoring the Duwamish Chief Seattle, a man indispensable to the early pioneers' survival. They, their progeny, and their successors made some things happen, while other things happened to them, but either way many of their stories inspire awe, others chagrin, and still others, simple delight.

For such a relatively young American city, barely a century and a half old, it's seen its share, and then some, of amazing events. Considering that when the Denny Party landed on Seattle's pristine shores, cities such as Boston, New York, and Philadelphia were already centuries old, what's happened in the Emerald City is remarkable.

It's strange that so many events in Seattle's history remain elusive even to native Seattleites. Do you think there are any Bostonians who don't know about a little dustup known as the Boston Tea Party? Of course not, but how many people in Seattle are aware of the Battle in Seattle? (Not the WTO riots in 1999—the one in 1856.) Do they realize how close the city's founders came to losing their new town? Do they know that there just happened to be a U.S. Navy warship with a contingent of Marines moored in Elliot Bay? How much of a factor was their presence in the battle?

This book will take you from Seattle's humble founding—and near losing—in that earlier Battle in Seattle to a dubious appearance in Super Bowl XL, which remains an odor most foul for Seahawks, as well as many NFL, fans today. Between these events we'll explore a wide range of spectacular events that happened, which have added color and texture to this far-flung northwest city's unique character.

Seattle's founders set the direction their new town would take right from the start. For the most part they were a tenacious lot with a stellar work ethic, which was often necessary to compensate for less-than-stellar civic planning.

For example, Downtown Seattle literally burned to the ground in 1889, resulting in Seattle benefiting from a civic "do-over," which upon retrospect was fortuitous for its development as a major sea-air-road-rail port city. Unfortunately, for many a motivated entrepreneur who chose to rebuild immediately following the fire, the city's decision to raise the street levels to eliminate the toilets backing up at high tide resulted in many storefronts becoming basements.

While this was unfortunate for 1890s shopkeepers, it proved quite fortunate for 1960s Seattle author and civic booster extraordinaire, the aforementioned Bill Speidel, who turned the city forefathers' misfortune into the wildly popular Underground Seattle Tour in Pioneer Square.

Through aviation, maritime, forestry, and computer innovations; the nation's first general labor strike; an industry-changing music revolution; civil unrest; and natural disasters, Seattle has emerged a strong city that continues to grow, evolve, and define itself.

People should know their history, not to dwell in the past or to castigate it but to learn from where they came, to better understand where they are, and to contemplate to where they wish to go. So, with this in mind, let's explore some of the fascinating events that have *happened* in Seattle.

# LOOK WHAT WE FOUNDED

## 1851

Much of this first event didn't actually *happen* in Seattle, but since Seattle didn't yet exist, that can be forgiven. The story of the birth of Seattle couldn't be properly told without conveying the sacrifices Seattle's founding Denny Party had made prior to its arrival in what would become one of America's greatest cities.

Originally, descended from Danish Vikings, setting Seattle's Scandinavian roots early, Denny's ancestors ventured to, and settled in, the British Isles. Now considered to be of English, Irish, and Scottish descent, Arthur Denny and his family may not have had a choice in their wanderlust. Like their distant Viking ancestors, the Dennys relished adventure and opportunity. Obviously saturated within the family's DNA, John Denny and two of his eight sons, Arthur and David, had an urge for exploration that would not be denied.

The trajectory toward a landing and eventual settling in what would become Seattle began with Denny's Irish ancestors' westward migration, from the Old World to the New World in America before the American Revolution. After brief stints on the East Coast of

America, the Dennys were once again westward bound. They eventually settled in Illinois, where John Denny became involved in state politics, incidentally becoming close friends with Abraham Lincoln.

The family's westward expansion obviously didn't stop there, and they were soon on the move again. Unable to deny that old itchy-feet gene in his DNA and enticed by reports from friends who'd braved the Oregon Trail and settled in the Willamette Valley near Portland in Oregon Territory, John Denny made the monumental decision to leave Illinois and embark on a treacherous cross-country trek.

Early on, the Denny Party, which included the Dennys and the Borens, had relatively smooth going along the Platte River. Later, when the party hit Wyoming, the challenges would increase as summer's suffocating heat descended like a wool blanket. John had tapped Arthur to lead the expedition; however, a recurring sickness placed that responsibility back on John.

Of great help to John was Arthur's younger brother, David. Nineteen-year-old David Denny proved to be the most physically capable of the party. He was the most skillful driver of the wagon teams and was their best shot, an asset that came in handy for providing food and protection.

Often seen while crossing the desert, which could cause the most stalwart traveler understandable consternation, were household items cast off to lighten overladen wagons, bleached animal bones lying on parched earth, and earthen mounds marking the graves of those whose adventure had come to a premature end. Disheartening though it may have been, the Denny Party continued on and, though the Rocky Mountains had been in view for a month now, finally reached the Continental Divide.

The party had achieved a great initial success, having crossed the desert without losing any people or any livestock. Arriving at Independence Rock near today's Casper, Wyoming, they found a sight that wouldn't be unfamiliar to folks traveling across our great nation today. Previous Oregon Trail travelers had painted or etched their names on the rock's surface. This gave the Dennys a great morale boost as it marked a significant milestone on their journey. But they still had to cross the Rockies and the Oregon Territory and, although they didn't yet know it, make one last push up Puget Sound.

Once in present-day Montana, the party had reached Oregon Territory, which at the time also included all or portions of modern Wyoming, Montana, Idaho, Washington, and of course, Oregon. At Fort Hall in southeast Idaho, the Denny Party, used to dealing with friendly Indian tribes, were warned about the hostile Shoshone people. The Shoshone had been attacking Oregon Trail travelers, often stealing their horses.

The Denny Party encountered hostiles only a few times, but at least one occasion was significant. Apparently, the comely Louisa Boren had taken the wrinkles out of one amorous Shoshone man's breechclout. The man offered Arthur Denny a number of horses for her hand—and presumably the rest of her, too. The warrior reacted so aggressively to Denny's rejection of the proposal that as soon as the miffed warrior was out of sight, Denny struck camp and put a full night's travel between them and the spurned would-be suitor.

Having survived the harrowing encounter with the Shoshone, and overcoming the daily trials of travel, they had at last conquered the Oregon Trail. The Denny Party finally arrived in the Willamette Valley (outside Portland). While John Denny's wanderlust was finally satiated, the same could not be said of his two sons. Arthur wasn't particularly challenged by moving into an area already settled and growing. His desire was to build a town out of the wilderness—from scratch.

Arthur Denny had first heard about the Puget Sound area near present-day Seattle from a man he'd met on the trail. The man had described the area's natural amenities in glowing terms, sparking Arthur's imagination. Having just come through a rigorous 2,000-mile trek west, he decided he'd now head north, tacking on another 175 miles. His adventure hadn't ended; it had just begun.

Arthur sent his brother David and friend John Low to scout Puget Sound. Along the way they met Leander "Lee" Terry, who accompanied them on the scouting expedition. On September 25, 1851, they landed at the headwaters of the Duwamish River, where the local tribe hosted them. David sent Arthur this urgent message: *"We have examined the valley of the Duwamish river* [sic] *and find it is a fine country. There is plenty of room for one thousand settlers. Come at once."*

On November 13, 1851, the schooner *Exact* landed with twenty-four members of four families comprising the Denny Party, at what is today's Alki, ready to embark on their goal of carving a home out of the wilderness. The pioneers consisted of members of the Denny, Low, Boren, and Bell families, aged from six weeks to thirty-four years old.

It must've been a disappointed landing party, huddling on the soggy sand and fighting a wind-whipped rain, finding David and Lee had built only one roofless log cabin. Apparently, the normally adept David Denny had fallen ill with the flu and, in a slippery-ax mishap, had nearly chopped off his own foot. Lee Terry was David's partner-in-crime, especially if crime can be defined as incompetence and laziness. The men had neglected to bring along a *frow,* a tool necessary for manufacturing shakes for use in roofing a cabin.

The families crammed into the lone cabin until others could be built. The epitome of competence, Arthur, of course, had packed a *frow,* and just to illustrate how valuable a tool it was, half the roof was completed in a day.

One magnifying glass through which we can look back to glimpse just what sort of people it takes to carve a great American community out of a wilderness is how Seattle's pioneers celebrated their first holidays. At a time when anyone would be forgiven for failing to observe any holiday, or perhaps give it short shrift, these folks did a remarkable job in making their first celebration one that folks would very easily recognize and identify with today.

Christmas came not two months after the Denny Party had arrived at Alki. However, several cabins were now standing, the largest of which belonged, of course, to Arthur Denny, and it was the one in which the fledgling twenty-four-person community would celebrate "Seattle's" first Christmas.

Does this sound familiar? Sure-shot David Denny provided two fat geese for the main course, and they purchased salmon and wild potatoes from their Duwamish neighbors. They made decorations from cedar boughs and wreaths out of Oregon grape (a plant resembling holly). Louisa Boren even used her own hair ribbon—a splash of red—to make the wreath authentically Christmas. Louisa's contribution didn't stop there; knowing they'd be celebrating their first Christmas soon after arriving in their new home, she'd packed some toys, which were given to delighted children on that December 25, 1851.

Following that first Christmas, in desperate need of cash for the new community and true to what would become the northwest's first primary industry, the pioneers logged the nearby forest to sell lumber to entrepreneurs ship-bound for San Francisco.

Although this was technically the founding of Seattle, the *official* inauguration took place on February 15, 1852, when, tired of dealing with the wind and poor port conditions at New York-Alki, the leaders of the fledgling community ventured east across Elliot Bay to today's Pioneer Square area. There they found much better circumstances, including deep water and a protected harbor.

On that February day the four family leaders staked their Donation Land Claims: William Bell and David Denny to the north (Bell Town), Arthur Denny in the central portion, and Carson Boren's claim to the south.

From that midwinter day forward, the pioneers would intentionally and unintentionally set the engine in motion that would create one of the most unique and vibrant cities in the United States of America.

# THE FIRST BATTLE OF SEATTLE

## 1856

"They wanted their land back . . . but they didn't want it back that badly," quips Bill Speidel in his book, *Sons of the Profits,* perhaps encapsulating that one-day battle launched by Indian forces to reclaim the young town of Seattle.

In 1856 Seattle consisted of about thirty dwellings, five or six stores, a church, hotel, blacksmith, and a carpenter's shop. The population totaled about fifty people; however, another one hundred twenty folks lived within a 30-mile radius of Seattle.

I think the battle's short duration makes it more interesting, rather than less. Although the battle's being brief is also what's likely responsible for it being one of the lesser-known general facts about Seattle's history. In fact, I learned of the event only while researching another event, which has also come to be called "The Battle of Seattle": the 1990 World Trade Organization (WTO) riots.

This first Battle of Seattle occurred way back in January 1856. It seems that rather than hostile anarchist forces, it was hostile native forces in an extension of the greater Yakima Indian War

(1855–1858) who'd arrived to stir things up. However, not everyone was convinced an attack was imminent.

From an account written by Rear Admiral T. S. Phelps, a veteran of the battle, seventeen years after the event:

> *The governor [Issac Stevens], recently returned from visiting the Cœur d'Alenes and other transmountain tribes, scoffed at the idea of Indian troubles, and on the evening of the 25th concluded a speech addressed to the settlers with these emphatic words: 'I have just returned from the countries of the Nez Perces and of the Cœur d'Alenes; I have visited many tribes on the way, both going and coming, and I tell you there are not fifty hostile Indians in the Territory, and I believe that the cities of New York and San Francisco will as soon be attacked by Indians as this town of Seattle.'*

Well, as it is today, when a politician says something, it's often prudent to expect—and prepare for—the opposite.

Upset at broken promises, broken treaties, and general political corruption, the 500 to 2,000 men of the allied Indian armies had decided that the whites, or "Bostons," must be exterminated.

In June 1855, U.S. Naval Commander Starett had orders to take the sloop of war *Decateur* from Honolulu, Sandwich Islands (Hawaii), to the northwest coast in order to protect non-Indian settlements from increasingly aggressive Indian forces. The ship arrived in Puget Sound on October 4, 1855.

It's hard to wrap your head around the mind-set of the settlers, which stretched from paranoia to scoffing at reports of hostile Indian forces marching on Seattle. In fact, only weeks before the battle, Seattle's contingent of Washington Volunteers, the local militia, actually disbanded, feeling secure enough that the *Decateur* and its crew of 145, including officers, sailors, and marines, could adequately protect the town.

Only days prior to the attack, a musket shot sent the crew of the *Decateur* to battle stations and settlers scrambling for the blockhouses built to protect Seattle's citizens. With no further shots fired, and no evidence of an attack having begun, an armed detail was sent to investigate the incident.

While searching for the cause of the disturbance, investigators came upon the corpse of *Decateur* deserter John Drew sprawled on Miss Holgate's front porch. It seems Miss Holgate's thirteen-year-old brother had shot the sailor during Drew's attempt to break into their cabin. Emotions calmed, but the atmosphere remained tense.

On January 21 an Indian ally called "Jim" informed Commander Starett of an Indian force moving west toward Seattle. Remarkably, many settlers remained apathetic. Fortunately, Commander Starett was more astute and listened to the scout. He also commanded an experienced and battle-skilled crew, which he deployed in four divisions, each officer responsible for a specific quarter of the town.

On January 25 Indians from the friendly Lake Tribes came into Seattle and received sanctuary because they had also become targets of the hostile forces for their coexistence with the whites.

The clouds hung low that quiet, misty evening. A sense of imminent danger threaded through each person's heart. Only an occasional barking dog broke the eerie, prebattle hush. Voices never rose above a whisper as eyes strained into the dark forest. However, as careful as the mixture of settlers, sailors, and marines were, some high-ranking chiefs of the Indian forces had snuck in among the "friendly" Lake Indians.

No more than an hour had passed when sentries heard a dissonant owl's call. Owl calls from both the right and left of the centerline answered. This announced the apparent arrival of a hostile force.

The chiefs had gathered to plan the attack. Those who'd snuck in among the "friendly" Lake Indians had, apparently, turned them against the white settlers. The Lake Indians were to prevent the whites from escaping to Elliot Bay.

Fortunately for the settlers, they still had a friend among the Indians. Thanks to "Jim," who'd given them a heads-up, the Seattle forces knew an attack was looming. The first person reported to have seen the enemy Indian forces was "Nancy," the sister of a friendly Indian known as "Curly." She screamed, "Kliktat," pointing east to men on the hill near Tom Pepper's cabin.

Ironically, the battle began during a loud altercation between unruly ex-Washington Volunteers and U.S. Navy and Marine Regulars at Yesler's cabin. At the height of the invective oratory, a ka-boom! from the *Decateur*'s howitzer overwhelmed the din. Indian muskets fired en masse, sending rounds zipping into the town like a hell-spawned swarm of hornets. Hideous battle cries emerged from the darkness, announcing the fighting had begun.

The first of three non-Indian casualties of the war occurred when a bullet fired by Klakum, one of the commanding generals of the allied Indian forces, and intended for Captain Peixotto, an officer with the Volunteers, struck a teenaged boy in the head, killing him.

The second came without violence and is a favorite story of the battle—one of those jewels that can be overshadowed by the larger account. A sailor by the name of Hans Carl, succumbed to an illness and died aboard the *Decateur*. The deceased sailor had been in the care of a young black man, but after Carl had died, the man left the ship and headed ashore to the fight.

Once ashore Lt. Phelps inquired as to why the man had left Carl unattended. The man replied, "I can't see no good watching dead man when Injuns is round; he ought to look out for his own self when fightin's goin' on, and 'stead watchin' dead body I want to do some of it myself, sah!"

In Phelps's account of the battle he wrote about this man, "The excuse was deemed sufficient, and his conduct, under the circumstances, warranted. A rifle was placed in his hands, a position in the line given him, and a braver man never endured an Indian fire in battle."

The third non-Indian killed in the battle was shot in the back when he left cover to get some water during heavy fighting. An unexpected advantage for Seattle forces was demonstrated in this object lesson in cultural ignorance: One shell from the *Decateur*'s howitzer landed in a pile of blankets. Several warriors danced around the shell, celebrating some spiritual "victory" over the whites. Suddenly, the celebration came to a tragic end when the shell exploded, killing at least ten men and wounding several others.

The ship's bell struck noon, and the final all-out assault commenced. The enemy warriors emerged from the forest emitting blood-chilling curses, in full attack. The South Division, only fourteen strong, managed to stem the onslaught of the enemy to within twenty feet of their line. The Indians continued firing but no longer advanced. One or two more surges and the city would have likely fallen, but those few Marines held their ground.

During this pause, reinforcements had arrived from across the sound to augment the position with much needed firepower. This gave the division time, during which the *Decateur* was able to direct its howitzer toward the Indians' southern assault. It also provided time to set up a field gun. Unable to counter the artillery, the Indian forces retreated and attempted an alternate assault route.

The Indian forces finally pulled back, and the last shot of the battle was fired at 10:00 p.m. The Battle of Seattle had come to an end. The U.S. Navy and Marines, along with the settlers, had saved the fledgling city. Miraculously, out of the thousands of rounds fired at Seattle's defenders, only two had found their marks. The Indian forces suffered approximately twenty-eight killed and eighty wounded. Only an estimate could be ascertained, as the Indians had left no dead on the battlefield.

It's interesting to note that on May 15, 1856, the captured Indian leaders withstood U.S. military court-martial in Seattle. With the ruling that the men's actions had not been criminal but had been acts of legitimate warfare, they were acquitted.

# HERE COME THE BRIDES

## 1864

Asa Shinn Mercer (1839–1917) leaned against the rail of the sloop *Kidder* and sighed; the end of his long voyage drew closer with each slap of the waves against the ship's prow. A chill night's sea breeze moistened his eyes as the ship slipped east over Elliot Bay's gently rolling waves. The vague silhouette of Seattle, the small Puget Sound logging town of about a thousand people, faded into view. The flickering flames of Doc Maynard's and a small greeting party's oil lamps dotted the shoreline. Mercer had accomplished his mission: With petticoats and baggage, the New England maidens in search of new lives—and husbands—were about to step onto the shores of their new town.

Asa Mercer achieved much success during his pioneering life. One of early Seattle's movers (literally, since he was the town's first teamster), among other accomplishments, people elected Mercer to the Territorial Legislature and, at twenty-five years old, he became president of the Territorial University of Washington. How had such a young man attained so lofty a post? By cleverly being Seattle's sole college graduate—he was also its only professor.

Although successful in Seattle, Washington, he'd eventually relocate to Cheyenne, Wyoming, where he'd gain prominence as a writer and publisher. However, the choice to leave Seattle wasn't entirely his own. In fact, if not for his brother Thomas, a judge, the Mercer name might not be so well-represented on Seattle area landmarks. But we'll get to that in a bit.

Unquestionably, there is one singular accomplishment that stands above his others in both fame and impact on Seattle's history: Asa Mercer brought lonely East Coast women to lonely West Coast men; rather than to the Territorial Legislature, if he'd have run for the position, he could have been elected king.

A booming community, 1864 Seattle suffered no shortage of loggers, miners, fishermen, craftsmen, and businessmen—with an emphasis on *men*. You've no doubt gathered a glaring gender gap among the residents of mid-1860s Seattle—tons of men, but few women of marrying age. Also, the families that had been established were producing children, who needed to be taught, and teachers at the time were normally women.

When folks consider what Asa Mercer did for Seattle, this old saw may pop into their noggin: "Everyone talks about the weather, but no one does anything about it." Everyone complained about too few eligible women in Seattle, but no one was doing anything about it. Well, Asa Mercer, a well-known doer, decided he'd *do* something about it.

Mercer knew very well where to find husbands in need of wives—they surrounded him every day—but where to find the wives? An educated man and logical thinker, Mercer relied on deduction. The Civil War had claimed hundreds of thousands of Union soldiers, many from the northeast, leaving war widows and eligible young women unattached. He decided to travel east to entice New England women to Seattle. With many husbands and eligible men killed in battle and others off fighting, unmarried women needed to earn a living. However, work was scarce as most of the textile mills had closed because cotton deliveries from the South had ceased.

From the pulpit of the Unitarian Church in Lowell, Massachusetts, Mercer cajoled the congregation with a special emphasis on the young, unmarried ladies. In the end he managed to convince eight women to sail to Seattle. One man also joined them. Mercer and his party traveled to New York, where they were joined by two additional women, a man, and another woman bound for San Francisco who would later change her mind and continue on to Seattle.

On March 14, 1864, Mercer and his entourage joined almost 800 other passengers aboard the S.S. *Illinois,* hoisting sails from New York for Central America. The ship passed through the Isthmus of Panama about ten days later. In Panama Mercer learned that the S.S. *America,* the ship to which they'd transfer for their remaining West Coast voyage, would be delayed by a week due to mechanical problems.

After a week's unplanned stay in Central America, the party once again set sail for California en route to the Great Pacific Northwest. Mercer learned in San Francisco that the monthly steamship aboard which they'd planned on sailing their final leg to Seattle had already left port. Not thrilled with another delay, rather than wait the better portion of a month, Mercer arranged passage on the *Torrant,* a ship known as a lumber bark.

The party first landed in Washington Territory in Teekalet (Port Gamble), on the Olympic Peninsula, to a curious greeting party. The next day they boarded the sloop *Kidder* for the final push into Seattle.

The *Kidder* pulled into the dock near midnight on April 3, 1864. The late arrival meant a small greeting party and a handheld lamp escort to Seattle's only hotel for the night. The next day the community held a reception at the university to show its appreciation for Mercer's efforts and to welcome the women who'd left their families behind for a new life in Seattle.

The first "Mercer Girls" to arrive in Seattle were:

Josephine "Josie" Pearson: schoolteacher
Georgia Pearson: schoolteacher/lighthouse keeper
Sarah Cheney: schoolteacher
Sarah J. Gallagher: university music teacher
Antoinette Baker: schoolteacher
Aurelia Coffin: schoolteacher
Lizzie Ordway: schoolteacher/school superintendent
Kate Stevens
Catherine "Kate" Stickney
Ann Murphy
Annie Adams

Mercer was emboldened but not satisfied with the small number of women who'd accompanied him to Seattle. The Puget Sound region's population had grown to about 10,000, and his goal was to eventually bring sufficient eligible women west, where marriageable men were plentiful. Therefore, Mercer headed out on a second wife-gathering venture, but on May 28, 1866, he returned to Seattle with only forty-six eligible women. Not bad compared with the first trip, but he'd promised the men that he'd recruit at least 500 women to embark with him on the S.S. *Continental* bound for Seattle. However, many "recruits" abandoned Mercer in force following a story in the *New York Herald* insinuating Mercer was engaging in "white slavery."

Still, at least Asa Mercer couldn't have considered the endeavor a failure. A *New York Times* reporter who'd sailed west with the ship to record the voyage reported that the normally stoic Mercer had invited one of the "Mercer Belles" to his cabin, where he'd proposed marriage. The reporter asserts the unidentified woman laughed at Mercer's overture. However, Mercer may have gotten the last laugh on the reporter; he soon married passenger Annie B. Stephens.

While many considered his procurement project a pathetic failure, having delivered forty-six potential brides when he'd promised 500, and taking one for his own, Mercer may not have. However, his own matrimonial bliss didn't go over particularly well with the majority of lonely loggers, seamen, and miners he'd "jilted." Let's just say Asa Shinn Mercer's getting out of Seattle with his hide intact is evidence that Seattle's sheriff, who protected Mercer as he departed, must have already been married.

# REMOVE YOURSELVES FROM
# THE NORTHWEST

## 1886

The knock at the door wasn't from a neighbor who'd strolled over to share a chat over a warm cup of tea. It was the angry pounding of a violent fist upon the rough-hewn door of a Chinese immigrant's shanty. The father sprang out of bed, and his terrified wife shot to the corner to join their two cowering children wiping the sleep from their eyes.

The father screwed up his courage, flipped up the latch, and pulled the door open. A large, angry man's lantern painted the frightened family with an eerie golden glow. In broken English the father begged for an explanation.

The man at the door screamed, "Out! You all have to leave. Get your junk together and let's git," as other men shouted similar vicious threats, ordering families in other cabins to gather belongings and vacate their homes.

The din of enraged townsmen rose against the protests of immigrant men. Crying women and shrieking children, the metallic and wooden clatter of horse and wagon, immigrant families frantically loading their worldly possessions, created a savage cacophony as thugs herded people out into the frosty February night.

These townsmen, many out of work, displaced by immigrant workers hired as cheap labor or as strike-breakers, with the frustration that an empty belly brings, had chosen bigotry, violence, and an illegal eviction to solve their perceived "immigrant problem."

Chinese immigrants to the United States were set up to fail from the moment they set foot on their ships bound from China. Intending to flee persecution, famine, and civil unrest, Chinese immigrants signed up in droves with companies looking for labor to build the railroads in America. All those folks who wished to come to America might have done better to adhere to the old Chinese proverb that goes something like, "Be careful what you wish for—you just may get it."

Railroad companies hired Chinese immigrants as cheap labor and often used them to break strikes, which may have not been the best way to endear oneself to neighbors in your new country, especially if you don't speak their language well, and you don't particularly resemble them in dress, manner, or features.

Chinese communities sprang up all over the western United States, including many in Washington Territory, where two of the largest were established in Tacoma and Seattle. In addition to working for the railroads, Chinese immigrants became the first non-Indian fishermen on the West Coast, and many were employed in the salmon canneries.

Another not-so-endearing quality, especially when job shortages occurred, was the immigrants' willingness to work for lower wages. (The more things change, the more . . . well, you know the rest.) Although not everyone in 1880s Seattle harbored ill-will for the Chinese workers, perhaps not even most, many did and they weren't satisfied to vent their frustrations in a civil manner. Unfortunately, they were responsible for one of the ugliest periods of hate and racism and one of the most shameful events ever to occur in Seattle's history.

On February 7, 1886, without warning, a mob descended on Seattle's Chinese immigrant community with a violent intent to evict every Chinese person from town. The mob came prepared with wagons, and once the immigrants had loaded their belongings, the mob drove them like cattle down to the docks, where they forced those who could to pay for tickets for passage on a ship bound for San Francisco. The mob intended that those who could not pay, a majority, also be allowed on the ship. The ship's captain didn't find that plan much to his liking and deployed his crew to defend the ship.

The sheriff and a few available police officers attempted to disperse the crowd and were initially repelled, but with the help of arriving militia, they were finally able to scatter the mob and then guarded the cold crowd for the rest of the night. The next day a federal judge issued an injunction preventing the ship from sailing and ordered the Chinese immigrants be produced in court to determine if their constitutional rights had been violated.

The judge had also hoped that the delay would prevent the mob from reassembling. A couple companies of Washington Volunteer Militia had been deployed to escort the immigrants to the courthouse. The judge inquired of the immigrants whether they wanted to return to their homes. Understandably fearful, most who'd purchased tickets wished to leave for San Francisco; they were escorted to the ship by one contingent of militia. The remainder were placed under the protection of the second militia unit and were escorted back to their homes.

Unfortunately for the immigrants, as well as the militiamen, the mob had regrouped 2,000 strong and became enraged when they saw the Chinese immigrants being returned to their homes; they attacked. The militia was forced to defend themselves as well as the immigrants, firing into the mob, striking five rioters and killing one man.

The Territorial Governor and the U.S. President declared martial law and sent a brigadier general and federal troops to Seattle to restore order. However, Seattle's militia and police had managed to quell the riot. Hundreds more Chinese immigrants fled Seattle, with the remainder under the protection of the police. Most members of the mob had also left under pressure from police and military forces.

The racism against Asians in general and the Chinese (by far the largest ethnic group) in particular was at a fever level. Following cruel incidents such as the Seattle riot and others around the American west, an "Anti-Chinese Congress" was held in Portland, Oregon. The corrupt result was the issuance of an edict "requesting the Mongolian race remove themselves from the northwest."

Today you'd never know that the anti-Chinese fervor in early Seattle ever occurred. Significant Asian populations now thrive here and elsewhere in the Pacific Northwest; in fact, aside from Asian Americans holding several high positions in city government, Gary Locke, an American of Chinese descent, rose all the way to governor of Washington State. From the early decades of the twentieth century through the present day, these folks have braved and overcome many trials to create vibrant ethnic communities and have contributed immensely to all aspects of human endeavor that have made Seattle a world-class city.

# BLAZING SEATTLE

## 1889

It hadn't rained during the first week of June 1889, and the weather was unusually hot. Anything in Seattle that was made of wood, which was nearly every building downtown, was ripe for kindling and prey for the slightest spark. John E. Back (known as Berg), a young man who some called Swede, was busy in Victor Clairmont's Cabinet Shop located in the basement of the Pontius Building at the corner of Front Street (First Avenue) and Madison Street.

Wiping sweat from his brow with a dirty sleeve, Berg suddenly noticed a foul burning odor. He quickly twisted about and found a gluepot he'd been heating on a stove had caught fire. Berg frantically retrieved a bucket of water and tossed it onto the flaming pot. Unfortunately, this only served to knock the pot over, sending droplets of flaming glue spraying out over the shop's scrap wood and sawdust-covered floor.

The flames spread at such an unholy pace that any attempt by any individual to douse the fire was folly. Berg and others within the building managed to escape without injury, although Berg indeed suffered after the fact when newspaper accounts blamed him exclusively for burning down the entire downtown, his employers canned him, and the young Swede was reportedly unable to find another job in Seattle.

However, Berg may have been responsible for giving the City of Seattle a blessing disguised as an apparent tragedy in starting the Great Seattle Fire. On June 6, 1889, the Puget Sound town was about thirty-eight years grown from its founding and was an emergent timber and port city. Ironically, optimism was the theme the day immediately following this disaster.

After the gluepot toppled and caught fire to sawdust and wood chips in the wood shop, a conspiracy of circumstances allied to allow the near-total destruction of downtown Seattle. By the time it had been reduced to smoldering embers, the fast-moving fire, assisted by ten to fifteen mph winds, had consumed more than thirty-two city blocks in the area of today's Pioneer Square, the railroad yards, and most of the wharves.

Among the circumstances: Almost every building in the city was constructed of wood, something not unusual for a timber town but still regrettable in hindsight. Fire hydrants were placed only on every other block, the water pipes were too small, and when multiple hydrants were charged, although there were four and a half million gallons in the water tower on Beacon Hill, the pressure was insufficient to fight such a monstrous fire.

Add to that severely dry conditions, an unusually strong wind, and an all-volunteer fire department, despite being reportedly one of the best of their day, rather than a prepared cadre of professional full-time firefighters, and all the ingredients for disaster had gelled.

In fact, when the fire initially broke out, the bystanders' consensus was that it would be quickly snuffed out, just as a fire to a similar structure had been weeks earlier. The firefighters stationed one fire engine by a hydrant to attack the front of—at the time—the only building involved, and deployed a second engine to the back, which was to pump salt water from Puget Sound. Alas, the tide was out—yet another conspirator. Oh, the firehouse would also eventually burn to the ground.

Remarkably, despite all of the flames roaring through Seattle that day, no human lives were lost, although one poor horse perished along with an estimated one million rats. (Perhaps you're beginning to get an idea of the earlier sentiment regarding a tragedy turned blessing; no one complained about this particular consequence.) Thousands of jobs were lost, and the total loss of property was estimated at between fifteen and twenty million dollars.

Another fortunate historical aspect of this catastrophe is that photographers recorded the devastation. Although most were preoccupied with saving their hard-to-replace equipment during the fire, at least one photographer snapped away as flames licked at the muggy blue skies, even as his own studio was threatened and eventually consumed by the fire.

Remarkably, this story is not one of disaster but a true American—or Seattleian, if you will—tale of perseverance; a northwest phoenix rises from the ashes. This was never as true as in the aftermath of the Seattle fire for all of the benefits it brought to the city. It's said that in order to have a strong structure you must first have a firm foundation. Well, if this is true, pre-1889 Seattle's "foundation" may have been quaint at best, but at worst it was pathetic. It's clear that without the great fire, Seattle would probably not have become the Queen City of the Great Pacific Northwest.

First, the fact that the citizens chose to rebuild rather than move to another location and start over is laudable and probably a testament to the Seattleites growing sense of self as a community. The motivation to immediately rebuild came right from the top: Mayor Robert Moran served as head cheerleader to reclaim the city from its ashes. The result you see today is the historical and immensely charming Pioneer Square.

Talk about unintended, or perhaps in this case unanticipated, consequences, the rebuilding began almost immediately, which they soon learned might have been less than prudent. Some challenged that they'd begin to rebuild as soon as the bricks from their buildings cooled, while others actually put hoses with streams of water on theirs to cool the bricks quicker and therefore begin their reconstruction that much sooner.

About six hundred Seattleites met at the Armory and with a unity rarely, if ever, seen in this town, officially decided to rebuild rather than move, but this time with an eye toward becoming a major city rather than remaining a modest timber town. It's interesting to note that a motion was made to rescind a donation of $585 from Seattle to the people of Johnstown, Pennsylvania, who'd just suffered a catastrophic flood. Those gathered overwhelmingly voted to send the funds regardless of their own plight.

One of the more important decisions was to create new building codes requiring brick and stone construction in the downtown core. The new platting of the city, which would now incorporate an area from Jackson Street to Union Street and the Waterfront to Eighth Avenue, would also widen the streets. The city created a full-time professional fire department with a full-time chief, while also voting to acquire the water supply from private entities and creating a public utility, thus providing a more dependable water supply especially for firefighting.

The fire created opportunities that no one could have anticipated or imagined. Within a year everyone who wanted a job had a job. Seattle's population had doubled from about twenty thousand to forty thousand, surpassing Seattle's neighbor and competitor port city to the south, Tacoma. And also within that first year, some one hundred fifty buildings were in progress or had been completed.

The largesse from Seattle's fellow American cities was inspiring. Tacoma sent her sister city $10,000, as did her larger cousin to the south, San Francisco. Other cities from all over the country also sent much needed cash, totaling some $120,000. Those in doubt earlier may now have considered the spirit of Seattle's modest gift of $585 to the people of Johnstown, Pennsylvania, a worthy investment indeed.

Bill Speidel, in his book *Sons of the Profits,* relates the story of a restaurant owner whose business was one of the first claimed by the flames. Well aware that folks would need to eat while rebuilding, he dashed several blocks away and offered to buy out a fellow restaurateur's establishment. That fellow, fearing his building would eventually be consumed by the fire, sold his restaurant on the spot. Unfortunately for the enterprising first restaurateur, the latter had made the better deal, as the fire eventually claimed that structure too.

The Great Seattle Fire was also the genesis of what's come to be known as Underground Seattle. Following the fire, although the city wanted to raise the streets in the area of today's Pioneer Square, they couldn't arrive at a decision regarding the specifics. (In other words, for city government, things were getting back to normal.) In the meantime, anxious to restart businesses, some entrepreneurs began to rebuild, adhering to the new setbacks for wider streets but not anticipating an eventual elevating of the street level. When the streets were later raised, this left what we see today when we tour Seattle's catacombs: former street level storefronts now basements, and previous second stories now storefronts.

The Great Seattle Fire may have destroyed structures, but it only served to enflame, rather than dampen, Seattle's entrepreneurial spirit. With an enterprising vigor, and with no tolerance for the thought of defeat, Seattleites drove their shoulders into the proverbial grindstones and built a sturdy foundation upon which to construct a spectacular city.

# DOWN UNDER—SEATTLE

## 1889

"Please, come in and have a seat. Go ahead, scrunch in there and really get to know your neighbor." The truly pleasant man smiled widely from a position surrounded by the eager crowd. Folks shifted in their seats and glanced around Doc Maynard's, a venerable old saloon in Seattle's birthplace, Pioneer Square.

People now settled in their seats, the host addressed them. "So, how many folks are from out of town?" Several people raised their hands. "Well, let's see who's come the farthest distance." Some were indeed from out of town but called out mostly towns immediately surrounding Seattle: Bellevue, Puyallup, Brier, and the like. One man was from Portland, Oregon; another woman said she was from England, but a shy woman in the front row announced, "I'm from Korea."

"Korea?" The host sounded surprised. "Well, thank you for coming all this way just to take this tour." Everyone laughed.

The host began his shtick about Seattle's history with a distinct nod toward anything that could humiliate or degrade Tacoma. Just then some attendees walked in late. They did that quiet, I-know-I'm-late-but-I'm-gonna-pretend-no-one's-paying-attention-to-me-and-go-for-a-seat-in-the-back dash for safety.

The host would have none of that. "Well, excuse me folks; hold up right there," he said. The new arrivals stopped in their tracks and adopted dumbfounded expressions as if to say, *you mean us?*

"You're late!"

The crowd laughed.

"Where you from?"

As if on cue the man said, "Tacoma." This evoked an even louder round of laughter considering the tour's undertone so far.

"Well, gentlemen, that woman over there came all the way from Korea . . . and she was able to make it on time." The place erupted in laughter, and the host finally let his Tacoma fish off the hook and directed them to take a seat. They smiled good-naturedly and sat down. People in the crowd, strangers but a moment before, were now murmuring about the joke, much more comfortable among their new "friends," and preparing themselves for something apparently different than the interesting but dry tour they may have been expecting.

"Oh," the host began. "Don't forget to hang on to your ticket stub; it's good for a two-buck brew back here after the tour."

The show prep was complete, and folks were divided between equally talented tour guides who could, and probably did, moonlight in Seattle's comedy clubs.

That a city as relatively young as Seattle even has an Underground City mildly reminiscent of those subterranean metropolises on the East Coast and in European capitals is enough to make a history geek salivate. Pioneer leader Arthur Denny selected the Pioneer Square area for what would become Seattle (a second choice after initially landing at Alki in West Seattle), disregarding its lack of level land and its proclivity for flooding. When the Denny Party first laid eyes on the shores of Elliot Bay, it looked much different than it does today. If nothing else, the history of Seattle is one of moving mountains—or at least big hills—and the moving began from the beginning.

Today the waters of Elliot Bay arrive in Seattle against a soft, crescent-shaped waterfront. However, when the pioneers first arrived, Denny's Island sat like a lazy turtle in Elliot Bay, the only level ground that was the genesis for what is now Pioneer Square. There were tide flats to the south where Safeco Field and Qwest Field now dominate the landscape. From the island, narrow spits of land extended roughly north and east, almost begging to connect the island to the mainland.

The tide flats between the spits were eventually filled until they finally united Denny's Island with the mainland. Further, the enterprising pioneers eventually filled the entire area, creating the quasi-solid foothold for downtown. However, much of the area was still prone to flooding, especially at severe high tides.

Seattleites learned to live with the soggy conditions, but they didn't learn to like it. It was especially uncomfortable for the ol' olfactory—the putrid smell wafted about when the aboveground, *wooden* sewer pipes backed up. I'm sure some townsfolk wondered if anyone would ever remedy the situation. Incidentally, some of these wooden pipes survive today, a fact disseminated by some Underground tour guides along with another more dubious "fact" that those surviving wooden pipes are currently in use by the City of Tacoma Water Department.

You know how they say some blessings can come disguised as a curse? Well, this is exactly what happened to create Seattle's most enigmatic tourist attraction. In 1889, due to a bunch of circumstances conspiring and then spiraling out of anyone's control, for all practical purposes, the Town of Seattle burned to the ground.

The conflagration began in one building when a flaming gluepot tumbled onto a sawdust-covered floor, but add no rain for a good week, a good hot wind, bad hydrant water pressure, and a large cluster of buildings made out of fire food, and Seattle was about to get a chance to correct past civil engineering mistakes, one of which was building on mud without proper respect paid to either the rain runoff from the east slope or tidal concerns from the west.

It's now legendary how quickly Seattleites set to rebuilding their town after the fire. Many barely let the embers cool before they began new construction. In fact, it is this singular ambition that set the stage for Underground Seattle. City planners had replatted the roads of downtown, extending the boundaries significantly. New street widths and building codes were enacted, and many business owners set to rebuilding their establishments, but this time with stone and brick. But what about the tides and drainage, you may be wondering? Yeah, good thought; even with stone and brick buildings the entire muddy mess they'd been dealing with would be repeated.

Some of the businessmen, tired of waiting for the city council to make a decision on a possible new raised elevation for the downtown core to the waterfront to assist with drainage, constructed their new buildings at the original street level. Apparently, this had not been forbidden or even discouraged by the city planners. However (you knew there was a *however* coming), the city eventually decided on a new higher elevation for that core of streets. They would raise the streets one to two stories above the original level. And so they unintentionally set the stage for Bill Speidel's eventual Underground Tour.

In order to accommodate the business owners who'd already built their structures, sidewalk stairs and ladders were positioned to allow customers access to the stores. Now, I have to think these were some pretty motivated patrons who were willing to first climb down two flights and then, having made a purchase, to climb back up with their burdens.

Obviously, this situation couldn't continue. If you ever take the tour, you'll see just by looking up to where the current sidewalks sit compared with where you're standing that a misstep back then would bring your shopping days to a quick and permanent end. The city decided the public safety risk was too great and they would raise the sidewalks, remove the ladders, and then seal the stairway entrances.

This created an interesting situation: Storefronts now became basements, and some second and third stories were pressed into service as storefronts. Of course it's not really noticeable today at the "new" (century-old) sidewalk level, but within the catacombs you actually feel like you're strolling Seattle a hundred years ago.

The Underground was actually condemned and closed off way back in 1907 due to public safety concerns, including fears of bubonic plague potentially carried by the innumerable rats that had reestablished after their population had been decimated in the fire. This left the Underground to the druggies, dregs, gamblers, pimps, and prostitutes.

Over the decades the area known as Pioneer Square swirled in a downward spiral of neglect and decay. Many businesses, fed up with the vagrants, vermin, and squalor, relocated to other parts of the city. So, if the aboveground was being neglected, you can imagine the Underground was perhaps not actually *forgotten*, because most folks didn't know about it in the first place, but virtually unknown.

Enter native Seattleite Bill Speidel, publisher of the *Seattle Guide*, publicist, and Seattle booster. Based on a totally unrelated incident in which some twenty-five residents filed a petition with the city in an effort to stop topless dancers, the *Seattle Times* published Bill's stories about Seattle's Underground to promote interest. It worked; some three hundred folks wrote to Bill interested in a tour of the

Underground. If twenty-five could move the city council to action in the case of the dancers, just imagine what hundreds could do for an underground tour.

In 1965 Bill Speidel coordinated with businesses located above Underground Seattle, and during the inaugural efforts about five hundred people paid for the tour. The interest in Seattle's underbelly had the tangential effect of creating an interest in preserving the more terrestrial portions of Pioneer Square. By city ordinance Pioneer Square became a historical district. It later became Washington State's first entry on the National Historic Register.

# THAR'S GOLD IN THEM THAR HILLS

## 1896

"Extra! Extra!" The young newspaperboy with the white cap tried to shout above the voice of his red-capped counterpart on the other side of Front Street. "The steamer *Portland* making way south toward Seattle with a ton of gold in its hold—read all about it!" The two boys yelled in unison. On the word "gold," conversations stopped and folks' necks craned toward the newspapers. People rushed the boys from every direction to buy the papers. They sold out their extra editions in minutes and flew to get more copies.

On July 17, 1897, the steamer *Portland* made its way south along the Puget Sound bound for Seattle. Those newspaperboys hawking that early "extra" edition of the *Seattle Post-Intelligencer* resulted in a throng of five thousand people to greet the returning ship, which boasted ". . . a ton of gold" in its hold. A ton—give or take, might be more accurate, as some historians write the amount was double, while others cut that number in half. Regardless, by anyone's standards it was a *ship*load!

Many prospectors aboard the vessel had returned to Seattle quite wealthy indeed, carrying from $10,000 to $120,000 in gold dust and nuggets. If you want to know what ignites a fuse to a gold-seeking explosion, well, sixty-four successful prospectors arriving aboard a ship, gold-dust-packed pockets bulging and gold-bar-laden luggage bursting at the seams, will certainly do the trick.

Gold fever struck hard and it struck fast. Incredibly, no one seemed immune. Seattle's mayor, William Wood, was away at a convention in San Francisco when he heard about the arrival of the *Portland* and its precious cargo. So affected was he that he actually tendered his resignation as Seattle's mayor by wire, and off he sailed for the Alaskan goldfields, dreaming of riches. Not far behind him were many previously stationary Seattleites: firefighters, cops, lumbermen, sailors, fishermen—anyone who wished to swap his hose, pistol, axe, or net for a pick, pan, hoe, or shovel headed north.

So, how exactly does a gold rush get started anyway? Well, if they didn't know how before, Seattle showed the world how to do it up right—and the gold wasn't even found in Seattle or anywhere close to the city. However, Seattle entrepreneurs knew there were two ends to a gold rush: There was the rush to where the gold was found and the place from where the folks—well—rushed. Prospectors had discovered gold here and there, off and on, around greater Pacific Northwest during the latter half of the nineteenth century, but the Klondike Gold Rush changed Seattle's history and set it on a trajectory toward becoming the preeminent city in the Pacific Northwest.

To see just how important Seattleites believed the gold rush's impact was on Seattle's success, let's skip ahead to a celebration that will give you the proper perspective. In the 1890s Seattle was suffering in economic recession along with many other American cities. So an event improving that financial status had a massive impact on the people of the city.

In July 1922 Seattle celebrated the Silver Anniversary (twenty-five years) of the Klondike Gold Rush. Thousands of people turned out to attend events, which included a two-mile long "sourdough" parade. The parade included floats as well as veteran "Klondike" prospectors. Folks referred to these Alaska prospectors as "sourdoughs," a term derived from the experienced prospectors who wore pouches containing sourdough bread-starter around their waists or necks.

The city featured entertainment including an authentic miner's cabin, shows, a Monte Carlo–style casino, and a fireworks spectacular above Lake Union. The celebration lasted for three days. Today, with Seafair, Bumbershoot, Folklife Festival, and too many other events to list, it's hard to imagine Seattle without some major happening every other month, but events were rare early on.

In fact, in keeping with how important Seattleites felt the gold rush had been, Seattle's first major municipal celebration, the Golden Potlatch, had also celebrated the Klondike back in 1911. Unfortunately, a riot at the third annual Potlatch killed a fourth Potlatch, and the event died off. The Klondike's twenty-fifth anniversary was too much to ignore and too much to resist. Nevertheless, after this special gold rush celebration, the city would not hold another major city-wide celebration until the 1950s, when Seafair was created to celebrate Seattle's centennial.

Many cities in the region, including Portland and San Francisco, engaged in a de facto conspiracy against Seattle's having become the jumping-off point for the Klondike. Each city's newspaper engaged in negative propaganda regarding Seattle, alleging everything from a lack of hygiene to a lack of honesty—"Seattle will cheat you" was a common refrain. Fortunately, Seattle had done a few things the other cities had failed to do. The first thing was actually a matter of geographical providence rather than human genius; of the major cities, Seattle was the closest to Alaska. Within the realm of human endeavor, though, Seattle entrepreneurs had opened mining equipment and prospector supplies businesses.

Seattle boosters also made a concerted effort to maintain relationships and correspondences with individual Alaskans. They'd also gone to great lengths to create and then foster U.S. government interest in Alaska. Following William Seward's purchase of Alaska from Russia, many people called the deal "Seward's Folly." Many folks thought of Alaska as a big, frosty chunk of frigid nothing. Seattle, instead, would have government officials think of Alaska as a big, yellow chunk of shiny nugget. Seattle also pressed the U.S. government to open an assayer's office in Seattle so returning prospectors wouldn't have to travel all the way to San Francisco to get their gold properly weighed.

In any event Seattle survived the negative press, and Alaska's done pretty well for itself. And if you visit historic Pioneer Square today, you'll find the Klondike Gold Rush Historical Park. This tiny park is often referred to as the smallest national park in the United States. However, it's actually one unit of several that comprise the Klondike Gold Rush National Historical Park, with sites from Washington State to Alaska.

Meanwhile, many who chose to remain in Seattle knew those riches were not exclusively reserved for those venturing from the city along that long and arduous trail to the Great White North. Those neophyte gold miners needed supplies—lots of supplies—for three years; trekking hundreds of frosty miles into the Alaskan or Yukon wilderness would demand it. Prospectors had to take enough supplies to sustain them as they could not depend on what they might find on the trail or in the field by way of makeshift supply stores and shady, fly-by-night vendors. If they figured they'd need it, they'd better bring it.

Merchandise flew off the shelves and out the doors of Seattle's shopkeepers, especially those specifically supplying the fortune-seekers with mining equipment and provisions. For Seattle the recession of the 1890s was over, and the recovery from the Great Seattle Fire was complete.

# THEY MOVED MOUNTAINS

## 1898

It was a beautiful day in the city by Elliot Bay. The birds were singing, the sun was out, and it wasn't raining. People were sparse in this part of town compared with the areas south of here toward downtown. No one seemed to find much reason to travel north beyond this point unless it was unavoidable. Reginald H. Thomson failed to appreciate the nice day as he stood at the foot of Denny Hill, staring up its steep slope. The young civil engineer had a vision for Seattle, but Denny Hill, and for that matter its namesake Arthur Denny, would block his vision, and view, for more than a decade. Thomson adopted his own version of a "Seattle-style" manifest destiny—a northward and eastward expansion—and it didn't include that blasted hill. Eschewing the curvy or hilly with regard to road-building—or city-building for that matter—between 1903 and 1930 Thomson's dream would be realized as what is still called today the Denny Regrade. The massive project eventually lowered the elevation of sixty-two blocks of real estate located north of downtown Seattle by some one hundred feet by moving sixteen million cubic yards of earth.

After becoming Seattle City Engineer, and working for many years to design a sewer and water system for the municipal area (much of which is still in use today), and after building for himself a reputation for getting things done, it was once again time for Thomson to tackle Denny Hill. One of the first things Thomson knew he'd have to do is convince property owners that it was in their interests to allow the project to include their land. Not an easy decision because it would require tearing down their businesses and houses, and then rebuilding from scratch about a hundred feet straight down.

Of course in the what's-in-it-for-me climate of early Seattle, a prime motivator was financial gain. That in mind, Thomson hired folks to do a bit of door-knocking, speaking with property owners in an attempt to convince them that the regrade would improve property values. He expected the business district, located to the south in the Pioneer Square area, to expand or even relocate to the regrade. Another fringe benefit he noted was that the regrade would remove the natural barrier that was Denny Hill and make travel easier between downtown Seattle and the presently remote Belltown, which was virtually cut off from the rest of the city.

While many residents bought Thomson's vision and agreed to relocate, some folks—there are always some folks—refused to move. Not easily deterred, Thomson went ahead with his plans, carving the regrade around those who'd been stubborn, leaving them, well, high and dry atop their own private plateaus. As is obvious today, even the holdouts eventually relented and sold, but at the time it created one of the most surreal landscapes in the history of American city building. The holdout houses were precariously perched upon odd buttes, while other houses had been rebuilt at the new grade in the valleys between them.

Not the least of these resistant residents was Arthur Denny, who'd begun to build a grand hotel on his hill but had to abandon it while it was still an unfinished skeleton due to the economic recession of the mid-1890s. Prior to the regrade, Charles Moore had acquired the hotel and finally completed it. He'd even constructed a tramway to transport guests, the first of whom was President Teddy Roosevelt, up Denny Hill.

Where Denny had been Thomson's initial nemesis, Moore had adequately taken his place. In 1903 Thomson began the regrade but was also intent on "regrading" Moore's tenacious hold on his hotel's lofty perch on Denny Hill. However, in 1906 it was Thomson's tenacity that finally paid off when Moore relented and traded his one-hundred-room hotel in the sky for one more down-to-earth, which is still located at Second Avenue and Stewart Street. If you're of an adventurous mind, you can connect to this early Seattle history by visiting the former Josephinium Hotel, now the Josephinium Apartments, appropriately located adjacent the Moore Hotel.

Thomson had been about half right with regard to his prediction for property values; they had indeed initially risen, but when the project failed to lure the main business district north, a different neighborhood "personality" took hold. The new enclave offered lower rents, which attracted what many viewed as a less-than-desirable class of folk. In fact, the city had hired a protégé of the Olmsted Brothers, the Boston landscape architect firm that had created Seattle's and Spokane's park systems, as well as their grandest project of all, New York's Central Park, to make a plan for the neighborhood. However, the city failed to ratify his plan, which, incidentally, would have included a transit tunnel from Seattle across the lake to Kirkland. It's also sad to note all of the view properties, hills not being a deterrent today with efficient modes of transportation, that Seattle lost in the "great" regrade.

The most startling items remaining of this historic project are the photographs. To view this portion of Seattle, with its now familiar landscape, in its unholy, unfinished state is nothing less than stunning. One photograph gives Seattle a phantasmagorical appearance, as if legendary fantasy artist Boris Valejo had lent his devilish brushstrokes to interpret a hellish Seattle skyline. The ground surrounding them having been sluiced, the remaining two mounds dominating the view are reminiscent of the buttes you'd find in a Utah canyon.

Study history and you'll read time and again hyperbole referring to men and women who'd figuratively "moved mountains" to accomplish their goals. Well, study Seattle's history and you'll find it's no exaggeration here; they really did—and often. In fact, over the course of its history, Seattle has built a reputation as folks who could truly move the earth.

Over more than three decades, Denny Hill would be razed and morphed into the Denny Regrade, an area encompassing roughly Stewart Street to the south, north to Denny Way, Lake Union to the east, and west to Puget Sound. The colossal excavation was done in three phases: Phase I, 1898–99; phase II, 1903–11; and finally phase III, 1928–30.

Thomson stayed up to date on the cutting-edge (no pun intended) engineering technologies of the day. One of those technologies was being employed in various mining enterprises around the country. It involved using high-pressure water powerful enough to move half-ton boulders to cut away the soil. Thomson correctly determined that this technology would work perfectly to cut Denny Hill down to size. With this technique workers eroded the soil, pumping twenty million gallons of high-pressure water a day from Lake Union and transporting it by cart, rail, and conveyor belt for use as fill around the city. About half of the sixteen million cubic yards of soil was redistributed within the site, while other portions were used to fill in the tide-flats area south of downtown, where Qwest and Safeco Fields now sit. Much of the soil was also used to create Harbor Island, which at the time was the largest man-made island on earth. The rest of the dirt was simply loaded onto barges and dumped into Elliot Bay.

Today the Denny Regrade is home to vibrant communities of mixed business and residential enclaves. From low-income apartments to exclusive condominiums, from bohemian shops to professional offices to the nightlife of Belltown, one of Seattle's oldest neighborhoods, the Denny Regrade remains a neighborhood in flux. But as the French novelist Jean-Baptiste Alphonse Karr (with a name like that he must be important) once noted: *"The more things change, the more they remain the same."*

# A WALK IN THE PARK

## 1903

Seattle's city parks story is not a haphazard one as it is in so many major American cities with parks placed here and there as land became available due to various circumstances. By contrast, Seattle's early pioneers consciously set about from very early on to make sure land was put aside for its residents, visitors, and posterity to enjoy. Because of this forethought, Seattle has some of the most beautiful and accessible city parks in the nation. This is due not only to the city's geographic location in the lush and verdant Pacific Northwest but also to those early Seattle city planners who felt that making parks *happen* was essential to creating a livable city.

However, let's not sugarcoat their motivations; altruism wasn't early Seattleites' exclusive aim. Anyone studying the birth and growth of Seattle would immediately gather that the American spirit of capitalism and entrepreneurialism was alive and well. Therefore, it wouldn't be far off the beam to speculate that the early focus on a premier parks system was also intended to attract new residents to the eventual capital of the Northwest. Regardless of the motivations, the results—a legacy still benefiting Seattleites today—are spectacular.

In too many major cities across America, municipal parks systems developed in a slapdash manner as land was donated, confiscated, acquired, lost, and then reacquired over many years. Unlike those cities, Seattle was quite bold in its land acquisition policy throughout the young city, even buying certain properties many people initially scoffed at, such as the Bailey Peninsula, which eventually became the splendid Seward Park, which is essentially a time capsule of what pre-pioneer Seattle was like. The people balked because they viewed the land as "too far out in the boonies." Seward Park has become one of Seattle's most popular multiuse parks and serves as a wonderful legacy to those who were bold enough to ignore the ridicule.

Another unique aspect of Seattle's parks plan was the notion that the parks should be interconnected by a system of boulevards and that no household in Seattle should be more than a half mile from a park. The city's borders have stretched over the years, but with mini-parks sprouting up everywhere these days, this remains the aim.

In fact, there is currently a city-endorsed movement to reclaim municipal rights-of-way. You know those pseudo-streets/alleys that long ago lost their battle with Mother Nature. Ironically, groups of environmentally concerned neighbors have organized to reclaim these bastard stepchildren of Seattle's "open spaces," from, as mentioned above, mostly Mother Nature. Their ostensible intent is to "beautify" these strips of land, making them usable to people in the neighbor-hood for light recreational and relaxational (made-up word alert!) pursuits. These reclaimed rights-of-way are not an intended part of Olmsted's original plan, although some may fit by happy accident.

Now, let's get back to Seattle's original parks plan. Seattle actu-ally created a Board of Park Commissioners way back in 1887, a mere three years after Seattle's first park, Denny Park, was dedicated on land granted to the city by David Denny. By the way, that park is still providing folks with a place to picnic today.

Although Seattle has grown by the proverbial leaps and bounds, John Olmsted's original plan remains a benefit to Seattle's residents and guests. The best way to convey just how integrated the Olmsted plan laid out Seattle's parks system is to take a virtual guided tour of one segment of the plan, from the Rainier Beach area of south Seattle. Hopefully we won't miss a park or two along the way.

First, let's note that some of these parks may not have been original Olmsted-planned parks, but they have been integrated within their original design.

We start at the Atlantic City Park in Rainier Beach. Next we come to the aforementioned Seward Park, which, among many other amenities, boasts a beach and trails for hiking through as pristine a Northwest forest as you can find in a city. In fact, like so many of Seattle's parks, it'll have you forgetting you're within the municipal boundaries of one of America's largest metropolises.

Next you'll pass the Stan Sayres Park and pits; pits, you wonder? This is where the hydros (very-fast boats) live and work during the summer Seafair races. But there's also a well-developed, well-used, and well-lifeguarded beach here. Head north to the tiny Bay Street Park, which is more parking lot than park, but it's interesting for its position on the lake beneath the I-90 Floating Bridge.

After passing Colman Park, we arrive in the Leschi neighborhood, where we find Leschi Park across from a marina and adjacent to a quaint (well, it is *quaint*) business district. Up the slope just west is the relatively untouched native wilderness of Frink Park. Immediately north is the popular Madrona Beach and Park, with fascinating landscape features rarely seen on a public beach, as well as a brand-new nature walk. Next is a more infamous member of the park sorority. The Howell Street Park has long been Seattle's unofficial "nude" beach. Fortunately (or unfortunately depending on your perspective—or timing), Seattle's climate makes the "nude" thing an intermittent, and temporary, phenomenon. Another small park with a big interest factor is Viretta Park. This little park bejeweled with large conifers sits just south of the house owned by Kurt Cobain, where he committed suicide in 1994. Many folks visit the park as a surrogate for paying respects to the enigmatic singer.

Denny-Blaine Park is just down the block with its horseshoe drive, at the apex of which is a low brick wall obscuring a grassy beach snuggled between some of the nicest homes to be found along Lake Washington. In the 400 block of 39th Avenue East and at the east end of East Lee Street, there are small, actually tiny, public beach access points. Next is Madison Beach and Park; the park has been recently renovated. Now, let's backtrack south and head west on Lake Washington Boulevard East, where you'll wind through the aptly named Lakeview Park to a great lookout point with a fantastic view of the lake and mountains.

About half a mile up the road, you'll enter one of the true jewels of the parks system, and one of the most recent of the Olmsteds' parks: the Washington Park Arboretum. This park contains one of the premier collections of North American, and nonnative, plants in the country. There's not much that grows anywhere in the continental United States that can't grow in Seattle. A wonderful new section even features flora from as far away as New Zealand. Washington Park also includes Foster and Marsh Islands, where you'll find one of the best and most accessible nature trails in Seattle, as well as the end of the tour.

Around the city the Olmsted Parks Legacy also includes Green Lake Park, where the lake was lowered to create an extra hundred acres of park. Volunteer Park began as a cemetery and is now a hub of the Capitol Hill neighborhood and home to the Seattle Asian

Art Museum. Interlaken Park just to the north is a favorite with mountain bikers, hikers, and skateboarders. South Capitol Hill's Cal Anderson Park (originally named Lincoln Park) recently received a face-lift and features excellent sports fields, meandering paths around grassy meadows, and beautiful water sculptures.

Revenna and Cowen Parks invite the multitude of north-end residents to toss a Frisbee or simply recline and enjoy a sunny afternoon. Woodland Park contains a world-class zoo, rose garden, and playfields. We certainly can't forget Magnolia Bluff with some of the most beautiful views of the city within the city. And while we're in the neighborhood, it's appropriate to mention the largest park by far: Discovery Park & Fort Lawton have a long and interesting history indeed. Once the site of important military installations, including a WWII prisoner-of-war camp and a strategic missile site, the military eventually ceded most of the donated land back to the city.

The secondary, but absolutely necessary, feature of the parks is the city roads that connect them. Olmsted designed wide and winding boulevards, which run through or alongside Seattle's ubiquitous parks. If you take the time to travel these roads, you'll surely begin to appreciate their designer's "signature"; there are definite similarities. For one thing, rarely are the roads straight. They tend to curve and flow along with the features of the parks they accent. A favorite has to be Interlaken Boulevard East through Interlaken Park. This road fits so well with the park, it's absolutely integral to it.

So, as you enjoy these many parks, try to remember they not only connect very conveniently with each other but they also connect you with Seattle's historic past.

# IN THE MARKET FOR A MARKET

## 1907

The day was as unusual as it was beautiful: bright blue skies above the glimmering waves of Puget Sound—Seattle in late May. The frequent gloomy, gray, mist-to-drizzle-to-rain had taken a rare holiday. Louisa held her little David's hand in a grip firm enough to prevent him from slipping and falling as she hauled him across the muddy street, headed for a vendor's cart. An avuncular man with a pasted-on smile rocked himself away from his leaning position against the dilapidated cart.

"Hello there, ma'am, and you too, little master. How can I assist you two fine folks today?"

The man was the epitome of over-politeness. However, his failure to remove his cap upon greeting them gave Louisa pause. With such an obvious slight to decorum, how sincere were his other manners?

"I see you eyeing those fat, juicy onions there. You have a fine eye for a good Sweet, good lady."

"Well," Louisa began, tugging David back to her side. "How much for a pound of your onions?" Louisa unclasped her coin purse and scanned its meager contents.

"A dollar per, ma'am."

Louisa's eyes grew wide below arched eyebrows. "My goodness! Did I hear you right, sir?"

"If you heard, 'one dollar,' then yes, ma'am, you did," the man said through his ever-present smile, which seemed to have morphed into a toothy smirk.

"But, sir, last month I paid only ten cents for a pound of onions. What happened?"

"Who knows? I'm just the middleman, ma'am; talk to the farmers."

"Momma, I want rock candy." David tugged on his mother's hand.

"David!" Louisa tugged back. "Mother doesn't have time for this right now. Mind your manners."

David pouted but knew better than to try his mother when she was in this sour a mood. Louisa stared into her purse and then out to the end of the pier at Elliot Bay, delaying reengaging with the salesman. The man, seeming to sense the imminent loss of a sale, kept the smile on his face for the benefit of waiting customers, but it had left his eyes.

"Well, ma'am? There are customers waiting."

"Okay. I haven't much choice, now have I, sir?" Louisa fished a dollar's worth of coins and then immediately snapped her purse shut. "I'll take a pound—please." The *please* was forced by habit.

This scene, one of many that must have taken place with the vendors who dotted downtown Seattle, precipitated the creation of what has become the longest operating farmer's market in America: the Pike Place Public Market. It's a market that wasn't planned for Seattle; it's a market that *happened* to Seattle.

Because of middlemen like the smarmy gentleman above increasing the prices of farm products, Seattle's early-twentieth-century residents grew tired of paying exorbitant prices for items such as onions, the rate for which had increased quite rapidly, going from ten cents to ten dollars per pound. However, the folks needed their fresh produce and other farm goodies required to enhance their quality of life.

Much of the animosity was directed at the farmers, but the farmers weren't too happy with the vendors either. After all, the vendors were making a greater profit on the stuff the farmers grew than the farmers themselves. So, in August of 1907, in a move that benefited farmer and consumer alike, if not the opportunistic middlemen, a group of about eight farmers drove produce-filled wagons from their outlying farms into town, where they set up an impromptu market at a pier located at the base of the hill directly below where the Market stands today.

With many historical places, if they are preserved for posterity, they often remain unchanged, museum-like, held in abeyance for decades or centuries, for those to enjoy a harkening back to an earlier time. And although we enjoy those types of places as well, the Market is certainly not one of them. The Market is a living, breathing, growing thing with a polychromatic personality all its own. In fact, this Market more accurately "suffers" from a terrible, wonderful, fantastical multiple personality disorder. Just stroll along its tiled walkways, inscribed with the names of myriad Market lovers, and tread upon its cobblestone streets between and among the washed, semi-washed, and—sorry—unwashed throng.

In a century, the Market has gone from eight four-wheeled, horse-drawn cornucopias tethered together on the waterfront to a sprawling conglomeration of commercial and apartment buildings, vendors' stalls, and an eclectic subterranean mall containing some two hundred businesses, almost as many craftspeople, and of course, about one hundred twenty farmers who rent daily spaces on the main level. All of these folks are attended, like remoras to sharks, by a couple dozen—and then some—of the most bizarre and sometimes unexpectedly talented street performers you'll find anywhere. And a bit oddly, many elderly residents call the Market's three hundred mostly low-income apartments home.

This Market is obviously fascinating, providing plenty of treasure hunting for the better part of a day. If you have affection for Seattle's historic places, you'll probably find more to enjoy at the Market than many of the others. Even if you're a person who normally eschews crowds, this crowd may not affect you like others. And the Market knows how to do a crowd, the Market being Seattle's number-one tourist attraction.

Although this urban marketplace is often crammed with locals and tourists, there is a disarming quaintness to the place. The worst thing that could be said of any vendor from whom you'll purchase a product is they were indifferent, perhaps due simply to shyness. Fortunately, rudeness is one of the Market's rare commodities. In fact, the Market folks are normally quite the opposite and some of the friendliest people you'll ever find in the heart of a major city.

In the end it's fascinating that the Market doesn't simply exist, but that the Market actually *happened* to Seattle, and evolution continues to happen. From its popular, although inauspicious, beginnings to its near collapse in the 1970s, to the thriving market we find today, there is no better representative of the strange combination of ingredients that make up this city, which is still striving to establish a firm identity within the quilt of American cities.

# FIRST IN THE WEST TO
# SCRAPE THE SKY

1914

A billowing white cloud blasted from the massive locomotive's steam vents, followed by a high-pitched whistle, which pierced the early morning quiet. The freight train, which seemed to stretch back to forever, paused before lurching forward. Chugging, clanking, and clapping, it tugged its burden faster and faster and faster with each exertion of its muscular steam engine. Three wide-eyed boys peering between the freight-yard fence boards sprinted alongside, paralleling the train until their little legs could no longer keep pace.

The powerful engine sped westbound from Pittsburgh pulling 164 cars, each loaded with twenty-eight tons of Pennsylvania steel bound for Seattle a few thousand miles away in the Great Pacific Northwest. The train carried the steel to the folks who had plans to build what would become Seattle's first skyscraper as well as America's tallest building west of Ohio. Using newly evolved technologies, which allowed the construction of steel-framed, high-rise buildings, the Smith Tower would soar well above any of Seattle's existing structures. These technologies included advancements in the ability to determine proper structure loads, safer and more reliable elevators, and, of course, the ability to mass-produce steel.

Prior to these late-nineteenth-century technological advancements, high-rise buildings were supported by the walls beneath each upper floor. For example, the ground floor of one sixteen-story Chicago building had six-meter-thick walls, and each successive story would be less substantial than the one beneath it, creating a pyramid effect. The new engineering technology allowed builders the ability to employ a steel "skeleton" to which the walls basically clung, allowing for a uniform wall thickness from the ground floor to the roof, and the ability to build ever skyward—or, since this is Seattle, perhaps ever cloud-ward would be more appropriate.

There's no way a skyscraper in a city the size of Seattle in the early twentieth century should have happened. Think about it: Even cities as great as Chicago, San Francisco, and Los Angeles had no buildings with heights sufficient to challenge Seattle's inaugural skyscraper. In fact, Seattle's Smith Tower would reign supreme in the west for many decades.

At the time, this new construction phenomenon, the skyscraper, existed only in New York, Philadelphia, and Cincinnati. And 1910 Seattle, while certainly a growing but modest metropolis, wasn't an obvious candidate for such a structure. However, Lyman Cornelius Smith, founder of the Ithaca Gun Company and Smith-Corona typewriter magnate, had a vision for such a building in Seattle. Unfortunately, although his vision would be realized with the dedication of the Smith Tower on July 4, 1914, Mr. Smith wouldn't be around to receive his just accolades; he died in 1910.

The Smith Tower, aside from being quite handsome, is an incredibly practical building as well. For example, how many people know that within the pinnacle of its spire is, or was, a 10,000-gallon water tank? You could look at that tower thousands of times over the decades and never imagine such a thing. Aside from the water tank, this top portion also contained a caretaker's apartment. The tower's water tank saw its last days in the 1990s, which is an interesting story in itself; what to do with a 10,000-gallon tank of nothing but air? Building owners decided to remove it, but how did they do it? Glad you asked. They actually dismantled the tank piece by piece and then—get this—they cut the pieces into segments small enough to fit in the building's elevators, by which they then removed the metal plates from the tower.

Today this top portion serves as a penthouse apartment (the only residence in this office building) with what has to be one of the best views in Seattle—that is, when there is a view to be had. And, as intriguing as this top portion is, the building is fascinating from its foundation up to its salmon windsock-flying pinnacle. First, the building sits upon 1,276 twenty-two-foot concrete pilings. Having the Great Seattle Fire of 1889 obviously on their minds, they built the structure with an eye to fire prevention. The first two floors are constructed of granite and the remainder is terra-cotta. The steel framing was coated with two inches of concrete, and adding as much to its beauty as to its fire safety, all of the common access ways are appointed with Alaskan marble, and the main lobby floor is tiled with sheets of Mexican onyx—very, very cool!

Advancements in elevator technology arguably allowed buildings to reach for the sky. While the structural technologies made it possible for buildings to go ever higher, climbing ten, twenty, or thirty floors and more wasn't something folks relished any more in 1914 than they do today. However, cable-driven elevators could transport people up and down with relative efficiency. But the elevators are not only an important part of the building's function; they are also an elegant part of its form. The building contains seven elevators, still serviced by human operators, which function with DC (direct current) motors—six of which were installed when the Smith Tower was originally built. (The elevator operators may not be the originals, but then again . . .)

Probably the most intriguing portion of the interior is on the thirty-fifth floor, which contains the China Room. The China Room was decorated with furnishings given as gifts by the Empress of China. The room's most famous, or infamous, piece of furniture, depending on one's perspective, is the Wishing Chair. Legend says any eligible woman who sits in the chair will marry within a year. No one knows if this legend is true; however, the daughter of the building's patriarch, Lyman Smith, married within a year of planting her own petite posterior upon the chair's plushy pillow.

The only reason a building such as the Smith Tower could happen in the relatively diminutive Seattle of 1914 is what had set Seattle apart from other cities of the time: Seattleites had a reputation for imagination and innovation, and more important, the courage to combine and apply these traits to make things happen. Just as after the devastation of the Great Fire of 1889, Seattle folks continued to look ever forward. In the case of the Smith Tower, they also began to look ever upward.

# LET'S DIG A TRENCH

## 1917

A warm afternoon salt-breeze blew in lazily off Puget Sound and rustled the gigantic oak tree's leaves. Ladies in their summer finery chatted while their gentlemen reclined in the oak's shade, enjoying their beverages, and children chased each other around its great trunk. It was the Fourth of July 1853 and Seattle was only a couple years old, but its pioneer residents saw fit to celebrate our nation's seventy-seventh birthday by coming together for a community picnic. Thomas Mercer, one of Seattle's primary movers, and perhaps a shaker to boot—and for whom a beautiful island city and a major Seattle street (incidentally, nicknamed the *Mercer Mess*) are named—chose this occasion to announce a grand idea. He gave what was reportedly an eloquent speech to the attendees, proposing the construction of a canal, which would connect the two lakes east of Seattle with Puget Sound.

Aside from conceiving of the original idea, Mercer's contributions to the effort appear to have been mostly ceremonial but significant enough that the results of his vision are obviously still with us and functioning superbly today. However, Mercer did rename the two affected lakes, which had previously worn Indian names, except for the big lake some folks called Lake Geneva. Mercer renamed the big lake Lake Washington, to honor America's Father. The new name Mercer chose for the smaller lake illustrated his confidence that the canal would eventually be built; he named it Lake Union. Unfortunately, the project wouldn't be initiated in any substantial way before Mercer died in 1898, and it wouldn't transport its first vessel until 1917. It would be more than three decades after Mercer's death before the project would finally be considered finished.

Early on, the U.S. Navy lent its considerable clout when it endorsed the canal project in 1867. The Navy was interested in creating a freshwater port for an eventual U.S. Pacific Fleet. They were very interested in locating that port in Lake Washington. Regardless, political dams mucked up any version of the canal's progress, forcing the Navy to consider other options. The Navy eventually bailed and chose Bremerton across Puget Sound as its northwest port.

Mercer's proposal of a northern route for the canal wasn't an exclusive one; there had been a few alternatives offered. Some suggested dredging the now extinct Black River, which served as Lake Washington's only natural outlet, by way of the Duwamish River, to Puget Sound. Others proposed a canal from Lake Union to Salmon Bay to Smith Cove and then out to the sound. The final proposal was a route cut through Beacon Hill. We can imagine it generally following the path that I-90 follows today. How different Seattle's skyline would be had that cut to Lake Washington been chosen. Safeco and Qwest Fields in Ballard, perhaps?

The U.S. Army Corps of Engineers, who'd eventually oversee construction of the canal and locks, endorsed Mercer's northern route in 1891. The Washington State Legislature finally concurred in 1900, but work didn't actually begin until yet another decade had passed, at last commencing on September 1, 1911.

Another reason this project took so long to begin and to complete is the massive scope of the work. Let's say we're standing at point A, which is at Puget Sound near Shilshole Bay, and we need to get to Lake Washington at point B—by boat. We'll first have to cut a canal through from the Puget Sound to Lake Union. Next we'll need to cut another canal through a land dam from Lake Union at Montlake into Lake Washington.

They also had to consider the water level difference between the sound and the lakes, as well as the need to keep the saltwater sound from contaminating the freshwater lakes. This necessitated the building of locks; the design called for two two-section locks. Locks are, well, just that, basically concrete boxes into which a ship will enter at one water level, and then the box will *lock* in the vessel. Next, water will fill or empty in the box to raise or lower the ship to the next level, and then *unlock* the vessel into Puget Sound or Lake Union.

Regarding the Montlake Cut portion of the canal between Lakes Union and Washington (and a *cut* is pretty much what it looks like), the ship canal's builders were assisted by two previous trenches dug through at this location to assist with transporting logs from Lake Washington into Lake Union. The first attempt was basically a little ditch dug by Harvey Pike in 1860–61. Strangely, Pike later deeded this land he'd gotten in trade for work done at the University of Washington to a new business venture in which he was a partner. The new company was called the Lake Washington Canal Company. However, rather than expand the trench or build a canal, they built a rail tramway, by which they transported coal from barges on Lake Washington across the marshy land dam to barges waiting in Lake Union.

In 1883, employing the sweat and toil of Chinese laborers, David Denny and Thomas Burke cut another wider and deeper channel at Montlake, but it still wasn't sufficient to allow significant marine traffic. However, it was a start and the logical location for the last leg of the ship canal project.

And what about the divergent water levels between the two lakes and Puget Sound? Dredging the canal resulted in the water level in Lake Washington dropping by nine feet. This led to some odd, some negative, and some beneficial occurrences around the twenty-mile-long lake. One obvious benefit was the increase of the lake's shoreline, as well as the addition of landmass to Mercer Island. If you ever enjoy the beach at Seward Park, thank the canal in Ballard for the pleasure.

Unfortunately for Columbia City, the decision to lower Lake Washington to the level of Lake Union made obsolete their plans to create a southeast seaport accessed through a ship canal using the Wetmore Slough. On the other hand, a whaling ship station at Meydenbauer Bay, as well as a shipyard at Kirkland, would become possible.

One of the odder things that happened was the exposure of a submerged forest of Douglas fir treetops in the channel between Mercer Island and what is today the City of Bellevue. Apparently, a landslide had occurred a few hundred years back, sending a portion of the forest into the lake. These treetops created quite a hazard, and an interesting obstacle course, for marine traffic through this waterway. Well, being timber folk, someone eventually decided to harvest the trees from the lake. Fortunately, the almost perpetually cold water had preserved the timber, which was extracted and converted to commercial use.

At the Ballard Ship Canal and Locks official opening ceremonies, which were held after some seventeen thousand marine vessels had already passed through the locks, the SS *Roosevelt* led a convoy of three hundred vessels of every size and shape imaginable in the procession through the new construction. The SS *Roosevelt* was distinguished as the ship Admiral Robert Peary sailed aboard to the North Pole in 1909. The locks were eventually named for General Hiram Chittenden, an appropriate choice as he was a tireless proponent for the construction of the Ballard Ship Canal and Locks.

# THE WILD BOEING YONDER

## 1917

July 4, 1914, was the date that hooked a young man who would soon change the world in more ways than could be imagined in the most fertile of minds. Pilot Terah Maroney had taken Bill Boeing, along with Bill's friend, Navy Lieutenant Conrad Westervelt, up for a flight. Soaring through the blue skies over Seattle filled the men with inspiration. In fact, so inspired were the two men that in 1916 they founded the plane building enterprise that would become the Boeing Airplane Company.

Private, pragmatic, a perfectionist: These are all equally apt and, you might notice, alliterative, descriptions for the man who started what has become the largest aerospace corporation on Earth. William E. "Bill" Boeing began life in 1881 in Detroit, Michigan, a city also known for big engines and fast stuff, but his destiny would be to change the course of a different city a couple thousand miles due west in the Great Pacific Northwest. Like so many others, Boeing would come to Seattle with one thing on his mind—timber—but would find his prominence and wealth in another area—aviation.

A private man, Bill Boeing enjoyed peaceful days aboard his yacht, the *Taconite,* sailing over the sparkling waves of Puget Sound. He specifically enjoyed sailing along the magnificent British Columbia coast. *Taconite* acquired its name from the source of Bill's pragmatism—his well-to-do German immigrant father, Wilhelm Boeing.

Taconite is the low-grade iron ore that had confounded Wilhelm's compasses while surveying the Minnesota timber acreage to which he'd obtained logging rights. Pragmatic as always—and in this case perhaps a bit prescient—Wilhelm had also secured the mineral rights. Prescient indeed, because directly beneath the layer of taconite, the earth secreted veins of high-quality iron ore. This pragmatism led to Bill's eventual inheritance of a million-dollar fortune.

Now, that's not to imply that Bill Boeing would have been less successful had he not begun his climb to airplane building dominance with more than the proverbial dollar-ninety-six and a tuft of lint in his pocket. On the contrary, Bill had double the qualities it takes to become a success in America, and it's obvious he'd have succeeded even if his pockets had been lighter. However, a change purse heavy with a million smackers didn't hurt.

Perhaps this story from the Boeing Company's Web site best illustrates Bill's penchant for perfectionism. According to the site, Bill's son, Bill Boeing Jr., tells of one occasion when his dad had observed an improperly fabricated airplane part on a workbench at the shop. Incensed, Bill tossed the part on the floor and stomped on it until it bore scant resemblance to what it had been. Bill Jr. added that yet another airplane part defect stirred Bill Sr. to declare, "I, for one, will close up shop rather than send out work of this kind."

Thus Bill Boeing infused his company, from the very beginning and from the top down, with an unparalleled commitment to the highest quality possible. When you think of it, of all the industries where the dedication to excellence is critical, there isn't one where it's more essential than in building airplanes.

The Boeing Company has long been an important engine of the Seattle economy, directly with its employing of thousands of people, and indirectly through its suppliers and subcontractors. There may actually be one or two people in the Seattle area who haven't worked at, or don't know at least one person who either works at or has worked at Boeing at one time or another, but it wouldn't be smart to bet on it.

Boeing has obviously built some amazing air and spacecraft and has developed some fabulous technologies over the decades, not to mention providing tens of thousands of jobs in the Seattle area and in other areas around the nation. It's no wonder that local folk are fond of saying, "If it ain't Boeing, I ain't going." In general Seattle-ites have a genuine affection for the "Lazy-B." (Oops! Well, there's another ubiquitous, although a bit dubious, quip regarding Boeing, but we'll leave that one for you to figure out on your own.)

Boeing is a portrait of the corporate never-give-up mentality. To say that Boeing has experienced financial ups and downs is to make one of the great understatements of the last century. However, despite many governmental and financial obstacles, Boeing has literally soldiered on. As a result, some of Boeing's more significant downs resulted in some odd ventures. When its corporate survival was at risk, the great fabricator of aircraft has dipped its giant toe into furniture production, managed public housing and mass (ground) transit, operated a desalinization plant, and built large farm irrigation and wind turbines. None of these truly panned out, but it shows a company's steel-hard commitment to moving forward against stiff barriers, not afraid to venture far afield.

On the other hand, Boeing has on several occasions experienced much success when venturing less far afield into more tangential areas. For example, when America needed to divert much of its industry to WWII, Boeing refocused its civilian plane production to manufacturing military aircraft. Boeing may have changed direction, but the commitment to excellence remained as solid as ever. Proof was in the creation of Boeing's legendary B-17 Flying Fortress. The performance was truly amazing as the relatively few surviving WWII B-17 veterans will attest. B-17s were so popular, many movies and television shows have featured this bomber as an essential character.

The B-17's performance wasn't the only thing extraordinary; the performance of the Boeing workers who built them was similarly stellar. At the height of the war, Seattle Boeing's production workers were turning out an amazing sixteen B-17s every twenty-four hours. Boeing's workforce had exploded from 2,000 in 1938 to 45,000 in 1945.

The roller coaster that is Boeing's history wouldn't change after the war. The company returned to building civilian aircraft and would soon bring air travel into the jet age. In 1961 the Boeing Airplane Company simplified its name to the Boeing Company. While Boeing had returned to building civilian planes, it did not abandon its military and government projects. Boeing continued its part in protecting America and its allies when it successfully developed the Minute Man intercontinental ballistic missile system, with their first launch occurring in 1961.

Boeing was also heavily involved with NASA, having been selected for contracts to build various stages of rockets that would send astronauts into space. And here's a surprise for you: While Boeing is synonymous with airplanes, the company also developed the Lunar Rover, which you may know as the dune buggy on steroids the *Apollo* astronauts drove while on the moon.

Unfortunately, Boeing experienced one of the worst of its intermittent financial woes from January 1970 through December 1971 when it was forced to lay off 65,000 workers—a third of the company's workforce. The Seattle economy being so tethered to Boeing, the unemployment rate rose to 14 percent, double the national jobless rate. The mood was so somber that bumper stickers on cars and an infamous billboard declared "Will the Last Person to Leave Seattle Please Turn out the Lights." Remarkably, this sentiment aside, while some workers did leave the area, the majority did not. They stuck it out, Seattle's industry began to diversify, and many workers were eventually called back to Boeing and enjoyed long careers with the company.

The Boeing Company can best be summed up with a brief cataloging of some of its air and spacecraft. Bill Boeing began building planes when he and a partner built seaplanes on Lake Union as a hobby. They then built the Model 40, which could carry half a ton of cargo as well as passengers. As stated above, Boeing later built the B-17 and also manufactured the B-29 Super Fortress, which carried to Japan the nuclear payloads that would end World War II.

Boeing built the 707 through 787 airliners, including the revolutionary, and instantly recognizable, 747. The company is also responsible for the B-47, B-50, and the well-known B-52 Strato Fortress. Boeing's contribution to military aircraft hasn't been limited to its bombers. Boeing also builds the Navy/Marine Corps F-18 Hornet and the Air Force's F-15 Eagle. And in the rotary-winged class, Boeing manufactures the highly advanced AH-64D Apache attack and the powerful workhorse CH-47 Chinook helicopters, the latter of which has been in U.S. Army service since 1962.

Currently Boeing continues to build some of the most technologically advanced and trusted air and spacecraft in the world today. With the acquisition of McDonnell Douglas in 1996 and Rockwell International Corporation the following year, Boeing has shown the world that it intends to remain the preeminent driving force in the aerospace industry into the twenty-first century and beyond.

# TAKE THIS JOB AND . . .

## 1919

A ghostly quiet blanketed the city this day. In fact, it was the *quiet* that most took everyone by surprise on February 6, 1919, because no one, and it truly appears *no one*—not even the labor unions who'd organized the action—knew what to expect when the first general labor strike in American history descended on Seattle.

The largest city in the Pacific Northwest screeched to a sudden and virtually complete standstill. The din of a great city goes almost unnoticed by its denizens most days. That is until the urban cacophony ceases, leaving only chirping birds and the occasional distant barking dog to break the silence.

Martha Boothe stepped onto the front porch of her Madison Street home and stood awestruck on this eerie midwinter morning. The trolley's clack-clack and chiming bell fell silent as the car halted mid-route as if some divine hand had stopped time. Jake, the newspaper boy, stuffed his papers back into his sack and skipped home. The clicks, squeaks, and hisses from the printer's shop across the street were as conspicuously absent as the clink of the blacksmith's hammer.

Mr. Lowe had left his delivery truck parked in the space it occupied at the stroke of ten o'clock when the strike officially went into effect. Mr. Lowe adjusted his cap and jacket and then sauntered off toward the nearest saloon, which, to his consternation, he'd find had also closed.

Martha didn't know what to think. She'd heard all kinds of rumors about what would happen during the strike. She'd heard violence was a certainty. She'd heard that roving bands of communist thugs would launch a mass berserker to destroy or confiscate private property. She'd heard even worse things about the roaming hordes of striking men harassing women.

However, only a calm sea breeze roamed the city. Quiet minutes turned into quiet hours, which finally faded into the first quiet day. The workers seemed to have heeded the union committee's call to avoid gathering in crowds and to obey police orders. Although one photograph from the second day of the strike does show a crowd had gathered, it shows no evidence of disorder. Written records report no mobs had descended, no property was confiscated, and no women were bothered. Milk for babies and medicine for the sick were still available, and the city's lights shone as brightly as they ever had. Still, Martha didn't know what to expect from the strike as it continued. She wasn't alone.

Ironically, the strikers and even the strike's leaders also had no idea what to expect. In a twist of timing, many of the city's union leaders were away to support a labor leader who'd gotten himself into a bit of a jam in Chicago. So when folks in Seattle called for a general strike vote to support the shipyard workers, although their own absent leaders and even the national AFL (American Federation of Labor) didn't support a general strike, a large majority of Seattle unions voted to carry it out.

This was a broad coalition indeed. From teamsters, carpenters, and mill workers to typesetters, musicians, and hotel maids, well over a hundred unions threw in together in the common cause. Even a

Japanese workers union, excluded from joining the Central Labor Council due to racism, joined in the work stoppage.

Being the first to attempt anything can bring problems, especially when you're dealing with something of such magnitude and potential impact. Some sixty thousand workers lay down their pens, hammers, and scrubbing buckets and walked off the job, effectively shutting down one of America's largest cities and the primary hub of the northwest United States.

The first order of business was to winnow down the accumulated mass of the various labor factions to a manageable unit in order to accomplish their goal (whatever that was, since no one had officially articulated any goals). So what did they do? What else? Like today, they created a committee. To be equitable, they initially allowed each union three representatives on the committee. With 110 unions— well, just do the math. Still an unwieldy number to be efficient. This number was again pared down to a much more practical fifteen-member committee. While the new committee was indeed more manageable, without a concrete goal they still lacked focus.

This lack of direction would cause the rapid rise of a flamboyant political leader and the eventual professional demise of a controversial newspaper editor. The story of the great strike was also the story of two individuals, each at extreme ends of Seattle's early labor movement. Seattle mayor Ole (pronounced "Olee") Hanson and *Seattle Union Record* reporter/editor Anna Louise Strong played important roles in the strike. Ole, a conservative politician, would declare himself "Savior of Seattle." Anna, an avowed socialist, encouraged by the labor strike but frustrated by union indecision, would define her side's lack of direction; wondering in print to where the unions were headed, she declared, "No One Knows Where."

Ole Hanson was a dynamic and opportunistic politician. In fact, some of his contemporaries described his speeches as nearly hysterical in tone. But while his tone may have seemed radical, his policies were usually competent and measured. Hanson had come to Seattle from Butte, Montana, having walked the entire 700 miles. This feat was all the more incredible considering he'd suffered a severe spinal injury prior to the journey.

Rather than succumb to the limitations ascribed to him by doctors, Hanson, an admirer of Teddy Roosevelt, who'd used exercise to extract himself from a debilitating condition, had fabricated a harness that allowed him to walk behind his family's wagon on their journey to the Puget Sound. After such a trek, it seems political wrangling paled by comparison.

After brief stints in the grocery and insurance businesses, Hanson found his success in real estate, which led him to politics. Elected mayor, Hanson publicly proclaimed himself to be a friend of labor, but when this inaugural labor action ended, he equally proclaimed himself to be "the man who saved Seattle from Bolshevism," the political movement then capturing a fledgling Soviet Russia. On the strike's third day Hanson spoke against the labor action, decrying the "hell-inspired doctrines of Lenin and Trotsky." He used his local and newfound national popularity to vie for the Republican presidential nomination. Hanson lost that nomination to Warren G. Harding, after which Seattle's former mayor packed up and moved to California.

On the other side fought Anna Louise Strong, and *strong* was an apt description for this early-twentieth-century force in Seattle. Although she was an avid outdoorswoman, at one time even spending months in the mountains, rather than physical strength, she relied on her intellect to promote her cause. And an intellectual she was, holding a Ph.D. from the University of Chicago.

Strong had long been an advocate for the socialist movement, in fact holding the Bolsheviks' Soviet revolution in Russia in high esteem. Committed to her political philosophy, she learned life as a socialist propagandist can be costly. Elected to the Seattle School Board, she was recalled due to her radical politics.

During the strike she wrote a widely read editorial in its support. However, as strong an advocate as she'd been, she wrote that the strike had no articulated goals, highlighting a condition that would cause America's first general strike to collapse, hobbling Seattle's labor movement.

A fan of the Soviet form of government, Strong longed to travel to Moscow, Russia. She finally achieved that dream and would spend almost three decades in the Soviet Union. However, following accusations of treason, Strong returned to the United States. She found that picking up where she'd left off in Seattle wouldn't be easy. Seattle was now a stable city with a content middle and upper class of both blue and white collar workers.

What the strike did accomplish was to show the ability of organized workers to shut down a major city while still allowing critical utilities and essential products to flow to its citizens. It also showed labor that without specific goals such efforts are wasted and can, as happened in Seattle's case, severely wound if not kill a labor movement.

When Seattle's unions decided to go out on strike, ironically most of them had previously negotiated good contracts with management, which is why the absent union bosses initially opposed such a move. The strike's timing was akin to using one's last match to attempt to start a fire with insufficient kindling and fueled with damp logs; without proper preparation, the fire is likely to die before it's served its purpose.

While the Great Seattle General Strike certainly wasn't the last strike to affect Seattle, it taught many lessons. That the power to shut down a city is a great but awesome responsibility, as the workers and their families also occupy town and will suffer as much, or more, than any employer.

# COP LEARNS BOGUS BOOZE BIZ
# BUSTING BOOTLEGGERS

## 1925

"Shhhhhh!" The big man raised a thick finger to his lips. The men accompanying him stopped cold in their muddy tracks and held their collective breath. They watched as the boss listened into the cool, dark morning, until his expression relaxed and he gave a reassuring smile. Clouds escaped into the cool night air when the men hissed out their breath as their boss signaled all was okay.

The water slapped against the side of the boats as the waves tossed them to and fro. The men approached the dock to unload the illicit cargo when one broke the silence. "Don't worry, Boss," the new kid said as he reached into his jacket pocket. "I'll take care of anyone who comes at us." He clumsily withdrew a tarnished .38-caliber revolver from his pocket.

With the speed of a striking cobra, the big man, no stranger to instinctive reactions during the course of his more legitimate "day job," snatched the pistol from the hand of the kid, who was ill-equipped to retain it. The kid recoiled, startled.

"What do I tell every man who hires on with me?" the Boss asked, unceremoniously hurling the gun into the lake.

The kid looked around at all of the other men who were nodding in knowing agreement. The new kid maintained a look of stunned disbelief; after all, wasn't he among a swarthy collection of "rumrunners" and "bootleggers"?

"I'd rather lose a whole damned shipment than lose a life—got that!" He patted the kid's shoulder and returned to monitoring his crew's efforts. The kid appeared about to protest but apparently thought better of it and set to work with the others.

Seattle Police Lt. Roy Olmstead had learned a lot busting bootleggers and speakeasy proprietors in and around the city accompanying the police chief's notorious Dry Squad. However, the lessons he learned would not be put into practice as one might have expected from the veteran cop.

Lt. Olmstead had moved to Seattle from Nebraska and began working as a police officer for the city in 1907. His two brothers, Frank and Ralph, also served in the police department. Olmstead had quickly exhibited all the qualities necessary to excel as a police officer. In fact, he rose to the rank of sergeant in 1912 and became the youngest cop promoted to lieutenant in 1919. Of course 1919 was the year Prohibition was adopted as the law of the land with the passing of the Volstead Act, or Eighteenth Amendment, which went into effect in January of 1920, something of which Olmstead was supremely aware.

Olmstead and his brethren in blue had already been enforcing alcohol prohibition for years. Washington State was well ahead of the national "dry" curve, having passed a state prohibition in 1916 and having already ratified the Eighteenth Amendment, which the state legislature had voted to sign in 1914.

When the federal proscription against alcohol manufacture, transportation, and sales went into effect in 1920, it was much more stringent than the state law. Lt. Olmstead was energized by the occasion and charged into action. He used his knowledge not to fight booze but to begin a bootlegging operation, which would eventually earn him the nickname, "King of the Puget Sound Bootleggers."

Unfortunately for Olmstead, he became an early casualty of Prohibition Bureau agents, who'd arrested some of Olmstead's crew and confiscated booze and property during a raid. Olmstead managed to escape, but the agents saw him, and the proverbial cat was out of the bag. The police chief conducted a brief investigation, after which he immediately terminated Lt. Olmstead from his position on the police department. Olmstead pleaded guilty to his crimes in federal court, paid a $500 fine, and was released to his own devices. The neophyte bootlegging entrepreneur was now at liberty to ply his new trade unfettered.

Olmstead then worked to create what was to become one of the greatest criminal enterprises during Prohibition. Unlike other parts of the country, Seattle was a bootlegger's nirvana: a long, mostly unprotected international border with Canada, a nation with a quantity of quality alcoholic beverages, a coastline dotted with inlets, coves, and islands perfect for evading Prohibition agents, and there was Seattle, a large city with a particular thirst in need of quenching.

Olmstead put people to work in every vocation imaginable in support of his "business." He amassed a fleet of vessels, trucks, and cars in which to transport his illegal product, purchased a farm to warehouse his stock, and acquired a network of distributors. He started a radio business (which eventually became Seattle's KOMO Radio), which he allegedly used to broadcast secret messages to his bootlegging operation. Olmstead was indeed a self-anointed king of an illicit industry. He held court with socialites, politicians, and legitimate businessmen. Circumventing Prohibition was often viewed as more of a quasi-criminal activity, as about half the population opposed it, and many of Seattle's most prominent citizens remained—if secretly—"wet," with Olmstead providing a much-desired product.

Olmstead lived in Seattle's Mount Baker neighborhood in a mansion called the Snow-White Palace. His enterprise was delivering up to two hundred cases of liquor from Canada per day, pouring into his coffers a staggering $200,000 per month.

But Olmstead's reign would not last; in 1924 one of his most loyal men defected and became a federal informant. That same year one of Olmstead's rum-running vessels, the *Eva B,* was captured at the Canadian border, its crew arrested, and its cargo confiscated. Olmstead's associates quickly incriminated him. Modern technology was also catching up with Olmstead. The feds had set up wiretaps on phones connected to Olmstead's business. The Prohibition agents gathered damning evidence.

In mid-November agents raided the Olmstead organization and arrested Olmstead and several of his associates. After his release, he defiantly, and arrogantly, continued business as usual. About a week later, at 2:00 a.m. on Thanksgiving Day, agents once again arrested Olmstead and his crew.

In January 1925 a federal grand jury returned a two-count indictment. This trial would be the largest for violations against the National Prohibition Act under the Eighteenth Amendment. Aside from Olmstead, the court returned indictments for eighty-nine defendants, of which only forty-seven appeared for court. The remaining defendants either made deals with the prosecution as witnesses, or they bolted to Canada. Some defendants had pleaded guilty while the court dropped charges against others, until the list of defendants had been winnowed down to a "mere" twenty-nine.

In February 1926, Olmstead and twenty others were convicted. The court sentenced former police lieutenant Roy Olmstead to four years in prison and assessed an $8,000 fine. Olmstead would serve his sentence at the McNeil Island Federal Penitentiary.

Aside from being the largest federal trial during Prohibition, the Olmstead case would be distinguished for another reason. It would be the first trial to involve challenges to modern technology applied in police investigations, and would have two of the most prominent legal minds of the day at opposing views.

Olmstead appealed his conviction based on a theory that the federal wiretaps, placed without warrants, violated his Fourth and Fifth Amendment rights. Supreme Court Justice Louis Brandeis agreed vehemently, and quite articulately, with Olmstead's theory. In fact, Brandeis made one of his most eloquent statements regarding the Founders' intent for the amendments in question. However, his eloquence was made in dissent, as the Supreme Court ruled 5-4 against Olmstead.

On the other side of the issue was another giant on the American scene; writing the opinion for the majority was the current U.S. Supreme Court Chief Justice, and former President of the United States, William Howard Taft. Taft's majority decision would hold up until 1967 when a Supreme Court decision, ruling that electronic surveillance was a Fourth Amendment violation, finally overturned the *Olmstead* decision.

Olmstead was sent back to prison to complete his sentence. During that time he converted to Christian Science. Ironically, the adoption of this new faith turned him against alcohol use. Olmstead would work for the rest of his life to help those afflicted with alcohol problems.

Olmstead was released from prison in May 1931. In November of the following year Washington voters repealed all of the state's liquor laws by a huge margin. In February 1933 Congress passed the Twenty-First Amendment, which repealed Prohibition, ending fourteen "dry" years rife with unanticipated spikes in crime and corruption.

Prohibition left a mark on Seattle, which could be seen for many years and even to this day. For example, it wasn't until after 1969 that a woman could even sit at a bar. And while wine and beer could be sold by the glass, selling liquor in this fashion remained illegal for years. Today, Washington State still maintains a monopoly on liquor sales.

Thanks to some diligent, and apparently effective, lobbying, Olmstead's wife convinced an anti-Prohibition President Franklin D. Roosevelt to grant Roy Olmstead a full pardon, restoring his civil rights, which also included returning over $10,000 in fines and court fees.

From all accounts Roy Olmstead lived the remainder of his life in an exemplary fashion, in the service of others, and well respected in the community, until his death at age seventy-nine on April 30, 1966.

# ROW, ROW, ROW YOUR BOAT—
# INTO HISTORY

## 1936

An early morning mist partially obscures the gothic Montlake Bridge, its twin spires pointing toward heaven. A thin veil of fog descends phantomlike into Seattle's Montlake Cut below, the final portion of the ship canal that runs along the southern boundary of the University of Washington campus, which connects Lakes Union and Washington.

The "Cut," as Seattleites affectionately call it, is an approximately quarter-mile slash through a natural dike, which once separated Lake Union from Lake Washington. The "Cut" began modestly in the 1860s as a small trench dug to transport logs from Lake Washington to Lake Union. Over the decades various projects widened and deepened the Montlake Cut to the waterway thousands of boaters and sightseers enjoy today.

It's not unusual to see all sorts of vessels passing through the Cut, especially during the summer, when they do so by the hundreds. What *is* unusual—well, for us average humans anyway—is to see how early—and how late—the Husky men and women crew teams can be seen entering or emerging from the Cut to and from grueling practice sessions.

As successful as other "U-Dub" sports teams have been over the decades, including its storied Rose Bowl and National Championship Husky football teams, no team, perhaps no other team of any kind in America, has so dominated its sport as has the University of Washington Crew. The team has led the field, but not just in the ways you might think, such as winning league and invitational competitions, international competitions, and almost too many national championships to count. No, this crew is in a class all its own.

Now, those things I mentioned above certainly do contribute to the tapestry of Washington's Crew accomplishments, but I'll bet most of you didn't know this little tidbit. At the 1936 Olympics in front of a huge crowd aboard a floating grandstand, presiding over which was one Adolf Hitler, the eight-man crew team from Seattle's University of Washington captured the gold medal for the United States—and they did it in truly epic fashion. In fact, in 1999 the *Seattle Post-Intelligencer* voted this amazing event as ". . . Seattle's defining sports moment of the [twentieth] century."

Any Olympic rowing fan in the world at that time would have been right to have expected that it was a supremely confident group of U of W rowers who'd drop their as-yet-undefeated shell into Lake Grunau. After all, the Washington crew had set World and Olympic records for the 2,000 meter during their qualifying heat with a blistering time of 6:00:86. However, the rowing gods must have been bored with these Americans, who hadn't a taste for losing, because if the Seattle team was going to win on this day, *they* weren't about to make it easy on them.

Best-selling Seattle author Robert Dugoni couldn't have written the story with more tension and drama. The American team's best rower, Don Hume, had fallen ill, was suffering from a fever, and had lost fourteen pounds off his already lean 172-pound frame. Bob Moch, the boat's coxswain, described Hume as virtually not present as the race began, simply rowing on instinct alone. The American boat was slotted in lane six, which was farthest out and in the choppiest water. They were so far away they couldn't hear the Belgian official giving final instructions. Not that it mattered since he gave those instructions in French.

The Americans became aware that the race had started, but only because they saw the other boats had left the starting block. Not a great start for the team, especially with two rowers taken ill; Gordy Adam was also sick that day. At 500 meters there were no surprises; due to the stall at the start, the United States was in last place with Germany, Italy, Switzerland, and the United Kingdom ahead. At 800 meters it wasn't any better for the United States, still in last place with the Italians having taken the lead.

Passing the halfway point, the Fatherland's favorite German boat had pulled into first with the United States still trailing all the boats. At 1,200 meters, with the American boat seemingly locked in last place, Moch considered changing the lead rower from Hume to another crew member, when Hume suddenly and inexplicably perked up. He began rowing harder, faster, and his comrades, now inspired, matched his increasing pace. During practice the crew usually rowed at a rate of thirty-five strokes per minute, pushing it to forty for training purposes. Now they'd increased their pace to a grueling forty-four strokes per minute.

At 1,500 meters amid the din of patriotic cheers from the predominantly German home crowd, the American crew of Huskies had crawled into third place, a half boat length behind the Italian team, and just feet behind Hitler's "Master Crew." The tip of the American's bow pushed through the waves past 1,800 meters and past the German boat, which Italy had just passed. The Washington rowers were rowing with every bit of strength they had. Their reserves had been depleted. No one could imagine from where the young men were drawing their energy. As their boat approached the finish line, somehow they managed to shoot past the Italians and win the race, capturing the gold medal for the United States. They'd won by a mere eight feet with a time of 6:25:40, a full twenty-five seconds off their World and Olympic record qualifying time.

Their oars finally ceased motion and dangled into the lake, not that the energy to effect even one more stroke as an entire team or as an individual remained within them. The boat drifted toward the dock and slipped into its birth. The men, aching arms dangling, limp, exhausted, barely had the strength to disembark their still-undefeated shell.

Standing on the Olympic Champion's podium, one can only imagine the immense pride and satisfaction the Americans felt as German Chancellor Adolf Hitler, Deutschland's presumptive fan number one of his supposedly superior Aryan crew, placed Olympic victor's wreaths on their heads and draped gold medals around their necks. Jesse Owens wasn't the only American to make the Führer cringe during the 1936 Olympic Games.

They often say that truth is stranger than fiction. Well, if Dugoni had concocted such a story out of his imagination, his publisher may well have turned it away as too fabricated, simply too contrived. This makes it all the more remarkable. It's truly amazing that the story is so relatively unknown among Americans in general and Seattleites in particular. Perhaps this telling has done a bit to remedy that situation.

# A LYNCHING AT FORT LAWTON

## 1944

U.S. Army Private Clyde Lomax was on duty patrolling Fort Lawton, a military base located in thickly forested northwest Seattle, when he made a gruesome discovery, the body of a man who'd obviously died by violent means. Although Pvt. Lomax was aware of the violence that had occurred on the base the previous night, this find would elevate the investigation of those involved to include murder.

There, not far from where Puget Sound's waves slapped at the edge of U.S. military property at what is now Discovery Park, suspended from a steel cable from a rope around his neck, hung the corpse of an Italian soldier. Although some officials initially considered Guglielmo Olivotto's death a suicide, circumstances seemed to make that conclusion a stretch. However, others adamantly believed that Olivotto had taken his own life that turbulent night.

Fort Lawton is a U.S. Army installation nestled on a bluff overlooking Puget Sound at one of Seattle's most beautiful locations in the Magnolia neighborhood. Hike the park today and it'll tease you with hints of this previous incarnation. Today, Fort Lawton still retains a small portion of the original land, but most of this former base comprises the largest municipal park in Seattle, Discovery Park.

Tromping in the park today, one can't help but feel as if one is walking through a ghost town. The forest slowly creeps across the fractured asphalt of roads no longer used as intended, threatening to erase its history as an army base. The park is veined with roads that crisscrossed the former military base, for which construction was started in 1898. The fort had been named for General Lawton, who'd been killed while stationed in the Philippines, but he had a more interesting claim to fame. In 1886 he'd led an American force into Mexico on a mission to capture Geronimo.

It's also amusing to note that the military's establishing a base in Seattle wasn't solely to protect the city from possible Spanish naval attack during the Spanish-American War. General Elwell Otis believed the fort was also necessary to prevent lawlessness within the "prone-to-unruliness" Seattle community itself.

Much of the land for Fort Lawton was donated by patriotic, if *unruly,* Seattleites. The folks offered up a huge parcel of land to the U.S. government for a military base. Although the base was used for many diverse purposes over the decades, for the sake of this story, we're concerned with its service as a prisoner of war (POW) camp during World War II, when it held both Italian and German prisoners.

Timing has as much or more of an effect on the fortunes of war as anything. In general the Italian soldiers felt fortunate to have been captured by the Americans rather than by the Russians, who virtually ignored the Geneva Conventions governing treatment of POWs. However, even in better circumstances, ugliness can still strike; after all, although winding down, the world was still at war.

What set the Italian prisoners apart from their German counterparts was the fact that in September of 1943, following the fall of Mussolini, Italy had withdrawn from the Axis powers (Italy, Germany and Japan) and from the war. This put the Italians in a sort of military limbo. There were some 50,000 Italian POWs, whose nation was no longer at war with the United States but was, nevertheless, not an ally such as France or Great Britain. What to do with them?

The military came up with a sort of compromise, which actually seems quite fair on the surface, but in the final analysis may have set up some Italian soldiers for abuse. The U.S. military created ISUs, or Italian Service Units. Captured Italian soldiers and seamen were given the option of remaining POWs or becoming "cooperators" with the Americans by enlisting in the ISU. These Italians wore American Army uniforms with the single difference being a green brassard with "Italy" emblazoned on it, which the soldier or sailor wrapped around his upper arm. Of the Italian prisoners in American custody at the time Italy's participation as an active aggressor came to an end, 66 percent of Italian military men chose to enlist in the ISU. The others were either loyal followers of Il Duce's fascism or declined for other personal reasons, and they would remain prisoners of war until repatriated to Italy.

Perhaps the Italians were inadvertently set up to fail due to the emotional effect on American soldiers, especially combat veterans of the Italian and North African theaters, who'd just returned from fighting the Italians as enemies. Seeing an "enemy" wearing an American uniform could be disconcerting to say the least. Also off-putting was the comparative treatment of those assigned to the ISUs.

Italian servicemen in the ISU received extra compensation in their paychecks, were allowed to live off-base and to go into town for recreation and were generally perceived as receiving better treatment than even U.S. soldiers—better than white soldiers. In the segregated American Army, black soldiers fared much worse than either the Italian or white American soldiers, perhaps elevating the discontent toward the Italian soldiers to an even greater degree among black Americans.

On the night of August 14, 1944, the black soldiers were enjoying their last night in Seattle before shipping off to San Francisco, where they would finally head overseas as a combat ship loading unit. The black soldiers threw a "going-away" party in their mess hall on base.

That night, four black soldiers confronted three Italian ISU soldiers returning from town, most presumably affected by alcohol. Historians writing of the incident seem to agree that a black soldier armed with a knife moved toward one of the Italians. The Italian avoided the knife and counterpunched Private Willie Montgomery unconscious. (There is some suspicion that Montgomery may have been faking the severity of his alleged injury.)

The black soldiers chased off the Italians with rocks and insults before carrying their comrade back to the barracks. Once there, word of the incident spread. Black noncommissioned officers quickly mustered two hundred black soldiers. An alcohol-induced rage ruled the military mob, and before reason could prevail they launched an attack against the Italians.

As it is with riots, collateral targets blend with the intended targets. Investigators surmised that at least one black soldier sustained his injuries due to "friendly" attack. White American soldiers also got caught up in the riot, not initially realizing the seriousness of the attack. They suffered some of the most severe injuries during the melee.

A photograph of the weapons recovered displays, among others, hunting knives, clubs, razors, rocks, and a hatchet. This collection of weapons was consistent with the stab and impact wounds suffered by the victims. Attempting to avoid similar injury, Private Olivotto was heard crying out to his mother and seen leaping out of a barracks window, falling to the ground dressed only in his underwear. Some say Olivotto ran off on his own and, so frightened, had hung himself. Other Italians reported seeing several black soldiers descend on Olivotto before dragging him toward Lawton Road. This was the last reported sighting of the Italian private alive.

After discovering the dead soldier, Private Lomax notified his command. An investigation, rife with charges of incompetence and corruption, began, although the U.S. Army did take the incident seriously enough to send a brigadier general to oversee the proceeding. The trial of forty-three black soldiers would be the largest court-martial held during the war. The riot had resulted in thirty-four wounded and one death.

Some charged incompetence or corruption because even basics such as taking fingerprints during the initial investigation weren't done, some of the weapons located at the scene were reportedly destroyed, and work crews repaired damage to barracks and other structures prior to proper analysis.

Regardless of the fact that the investigation seems to have been flawed, a large contingent of black soldiers attacked the Italians, and aside from whether Olivotto was lynched or committed suicide, which seems highly unlikely under the circumstances, many Italian and white American soldiers suffered very serious injuries, including broken bones, knife wounds, and a fractured skull.

However, the Army at the time was notorious for its treatment of black soldiers in general. So it's not a stretch that some soldiers may have been caught up in the riot and falsely accused and convicted of crimes, which led to prison sentences and dishonorable discharges. Fortunately, although mostly symbolic, especially for the families of those veterans who've already passed on, a wrong may have been righted when officials held a ceremony at Fort Lawton on July 26, 2008, formally apologizing to the families of three convicted soldiers and to Samuel Snow, a surviving convicted soldier. Although Snow had been able to make the trip from Florida, illness prevented him from attending the ceremonies. Snow died shortly after the ceremony and after the Army had upgraded his dishonorable discharge to an honorable discharge.

# MYSTERIES OF THE DEEP

## 1942

A generous summer breeze filled the fluttering sail of the boat, propelling it over the sparkling waves of the lake. The wind whipped against the passengers and sprayed droplets of refreshing water into their faces, a cool respite from the August heat.

Out for a pleasant day on the east side of Lake Washington, Paul Moran and other passengers had been enjoying a ride aboard a sailboat when, from their vantage cruising the bay between Champagne Point and Juanita, they noticed something very wrong in the sky. Moran gazed in horror as a torpedo bomber on a training mission out of Sand Point Naval Air Station spun out of control, slammed into the lake, and broke into pieces, hurling one of the fliers into the air.

The sailors rushed to the crash scene to check for survivors. They found two downed fliers and assisted them until a crew from the Navy responded from Sand Point to rescue the airmen. Moran also reported that the Navy had later dispatched a crane barge to the area over the wreckage. He assumed they were attempting to recover the plane and one crewman who'd perished, but he hadn't observed them actually recover any items. A U.S. Navy spokesperson stated they'd found no records indicating a successful retrieval at the crash site, but added that didn't mean that nothing had been recovered.

Many historic events have occurred at Sand Point (now Magnuson Park and a National Oceanic & Atmospheric Administration (NOAA) facility) over the years, planned and unplanned. Planned events at Sand Point include the first aerial circumnavigation of the globe, which began on April 6, 1924, and ended 30,000 miles later on September 28, 1924; a stopover by Charles Lindbergh in the historic *Spirit of St. Louis* (a plane especially popular in Seattle as it was made almost exclusively of Washington western cedar) on September 13, 1927; and, for our interest in this story, a stint as a U.S. Naval Air Station, one of only five in the nation at the time of its dedication. It's this incarnation as a WWII military airbase that has left the longest legacy in the form of a few mysteries, some of which remain to this day.

Today this stretch of land in northeast Seattle, formerly known as Naval Air Station (NAS) Seattle, primarily serves the community as Magnuson Park, a large city park bejeweled with artwork throughout, a fine kite-flying knoll, and one of the most accessible boat launches in the city, not to mention the NOAA facility with its own distinguished art walk. The park has a unique landscape, having an almost arid appearance. And for anyplace in Seattle, dry is odd to say the least.

However, the clues that whisper back from its days as an airbase abound. Cracked and weed-strewn concrete bunkers and portions of former runways, which now serve as park roadways, remain as subtle but fascinating evidence of its prior service. After the horror of the attack on Pearl Harbor and America's declaration of war against the Japanese Empire, the Navy needed fighter pilots for action in the Pacific Theater. Many of these combat pilots were trained at NAS Sand Point. It would be easy for Seattleites who spend so much time on and around Lake Washington, or especially living within a few miles of its shore, to look up and imagine the WWII fighters ripping across the blue skies or, more often than not, tearing through its gray clouds as Navy fighter pilots trained for future dogfights over the South Pacific.

It was during one of these training exercises that a terrible incident would occur and then remain a mystery for over six decades. The primary fighter aircraft of the day, based at Sand Point, was the Grumman TBF-1 Avenger torpedo bomber, a plane so named for America's desire to avenge the Japanese attack on Hawaii.

The Avenger was a formidable plane, which served in the skies both over Europe and the Pacific. This aircraft was a compact powerhouse capable of carrying two thousand pounds of bombs or one torpedo. Add to that three machine guns and you've got a fighter you're happy to have on *your* side. The fighter had two 30-caliber guns, one fired forward from the engine cowling, the other from the ventral position, or underbelly, and a 50-caliber gun was mounted in a turret in the dorsal position. The Avengers were responsible for devastating attacks on Axis oil refineries and German and Japanese ships.

The Avenger's wingspan stretched across about fifty-five feet, and from prop to tail it measured a bit longer than forty feet. It could soar to an altitude of 22,400 feet and had a range of 1,215 miles. The fighter normally cruised at 145 mph but would top out blasting to 276 mph bursts of speed. Depending on ordnance, she scaled between a lithe five and lean seven and a half tons.

Now that you're acquainted with this fine piece of aviation engineering, here's a story about at least one of them. On August 17, 1942, four Avenger torpedo bombers left Sand Point Naval Air Station for mock combat exercises over Lake Washington. Their mission was to attack a simulated target located near Meydenbauer Bay off the

Bellevue shoreline. The squadron of fighters roared over the waves, zeroing in on their targets, pushing 200 knots (about 230 mph).

To add realism to the simulation, three Grumman Navy/Marine F4F Wildcats sped in toward the target from the opposite direction at a good 300 knots. Tragically, one of the Wildcat pilots neglected to pull up in time and collided with one of the Avengers. The Wildcat arced over toward the west side of the lake and slammed into the water near Leschi—that pilot managed to escape. The Avenger headed north, presumably attempting to return to Sand Point. The pilot lowered the landing gear to slow the plane, and he bailed out. Unfortunately, the radioman/ventral gunner was trapped and drowned within the wreckage when the plane crashed.

Over the years folks have attempted to locate the wreckage of the Avenger, but they were looking for an entire submerged craft. They may not have considered that the plane had broken up and may have overlooked individual parts of the plane scattered on the lake bed.

After six decades of eluding explorers, on October 4, 2004, Crayton Fenn and John Sharps of SCRET (Submerged Cultural Resources Exploration Team), using high resolution sonar, finally glimpsed portions of the Avenger lying at the bottom of Lake Washington. With their imaging technology they were able to capture views of three major portions of the aircraft—the fuselage and one wing, the other wing, and the tail section—which had apparently been separated in the crash.

Having these images, they put together a team and sent divers below to photograph the wreckage. Their obvious success, along with some remarkable photographs, is documented at their Web site, www.scret.org.

Much of the mystery has been solved, primarily that the craft was at the bottom of the lake at all. However, some secrets remain. For example, two large sections of the plane have not been found among the other pieces. And these are not insignificant parts. For one, the entire front portion of the plane, including the engine and propeller, are missing, as well as the fuselage portion from aft of the dorsal turret back to just fore of the tail section.

Speculation is that the Navy had indeed recovered portions of the plane back in 1942, perhaps the engine, which it used to help to determine the cause of the crash. As for the aft fuselage, this portion contained the ventral turret, which would have held the remains of the gunner who'd reportedly been trapped at the time it plunged into the lake. Perhaps the Navy had been able to recover its flier and properly commend his spirit to the next life as the hero surely deserved.

# SEATTLE, MEET THE WORLD

## 1962

You don't one day just up and declare, "Hey, let's have a world's fair." It just doesn't happen that way—or does it? Well, perhaps for most of us it might not work out that way, but for one man, his memories of a singular event he'd attended as a boy would cause him to do just that.

✣

"Dang it!" young Al said. His head whipped to and fro, hopeful no one had heard his exclamation. A loaf of partially done bread had gummed up the bread-slicer again. But Al didn't care; his Sunday school teacher had hired him to help her at a tearoom at the fairgrounds. The tearoom was short-lived, but Al didn't mind much because the event he'd dreamed about had finally arrived: The 1909 Alaska-Yukon-Pacific (A-Y-P) Exposition was open at last.

Originally the fair was intended to honor the tenth anniversary of the day prospectors brought the first Klondike gold shipments to Seattle. The new University of Washington campus had been constructed for the fair and featured wide-ranging exhibits and vendors that attracted some three and a half million attendees. One of those attendees, the fourteen-year-old Al Rochester, had received an employee's pass, which allowed him free entry to the exhibition grounds.

That morning Al had streaked across the kitchen, anxious to get to the fairgrounds. "Slow down, Attie Boy!" his mother shouted. "You'll kill yourself before you even get there." Al shot out of their Fifteenth Avenue East house, raced down the steps, and ran across the street into Volunteer Park.

"Be good." His mother's now faint voice faded in the distance. He dashed across a broad lawn and disappeared over the crown of the hill, a two-legged missile headed toward the exhibition grounds.

Al proudly displayed his pass and entered the fairgrounds.

"Hey, kid!" a man with the face of a weasel called to Al. "You want to make some money, kid? Of course you do," the man said. "Come over here." Al sidled over to the man, who slipped his arm around the boy, his bony fingers draped over Al's shoulder.

"What do I have to do?" Al asked.

The weasely-faced man grinned, glanced around, and then whispered in Al's ear while pointing to various exhibits.

A moment later Al cried out, "Holy cow, this is amazing!" Al pointed in exaggerated awe at this booth and that exhibit before he'd dash to the ticket booth. Bystanders, caught up in Al's youthful exuberance, chased after him, now eager to buy tickets.

‡

So what does this all have to do with Seattle's 1962 World's Fair (also known as the Century 21 Exposition)? Well, if it weren't for young Al's experiences at the A-Y-P, it's quite likely there never would have been a World's Fair, and the City of Seattle may not have risen to become the crown jewel of the Pacific Northwest. The

Seattle World's Fair slapped the city prominently on the map and introduced her in glowing terms to the world. Seattle had what is arguably America's most well-known World's Fair, in part due to the legacy of the structures and features that remain today as well-used facilities such as the Monorail and the city's most recognizable landmark, the Space Needle.

Al grew up, fought in World War I, and then returned home to become quite successful, even earning a seat on the Seattle City Council. Although Al probably masticated on the idea of hosting a world's fair in Seattle within the chambers of his own mind, in the early 1950s he decided to finally make his idea public. The post-WWII business boom had begun to flag, so the timing was good. Also, he could take advantage of the fiftieth anniversary of the A-Y-P in 1959, which was fast approaching.

In January of 1955 Al first publicly broached the subject of bringing a World's Fair to Seattle. He was enjoying a casual luncheon with three influential business buddies at the Washington Athletic Club. Al's buds enthusiastically endorsed the idea. I imagine it was a giddy Al who'd returned to his city hall office to transfer the idea from his head to words on a page. He drafted a memorandum to the Washington State Legislature officially proposing Seattle host a World's Fair.

As with all big ideas, saying you're going to do it is a heck of a lot easier than doing it. For one thing, in order for the event to be a legitimate World's Fair, which would attract participation from around the globe, it would have to be officially sanctioned. However, the sanctioning body, the Bureau of International Exposition (BIE), located in Paris, France, wasn't about to bestow such an accreditation easily, especially on a city few outside of America had heard of. And besides, there was still another obstacle: New York City's name was also in the hat.

What were the chances for little-known, Podunk Seattle up against mighty Gotham, the Big Apple, perhaps the greatest city on earth? It didn't look too good for the awkward upstart from the Evergreen State. Even the members of the BIE mispronounced Seattle, pronouncing it "See-tull." To them, Seattle, or *See-tull*, was a suburban city located near the *other* Washington—D.C.

However, according to BIE officials, the New Yorkers were brash and condescending, while the Seattleites were polite and accommodating. It was the do-you-know-who-we-are East Coasters vs. the aw-shucks West Coasters. Well, the Seattleite's good manners paid off with BIE credentials issued in November 1960.

Having the credentials was great, but it wasn't even half the battle. They still needed to attract world interest in sponsoring exhibits, obtain land for the fairgrounds, and develop their own themes and homegrown attractions.

With the paperwork in order, they now needed to actually build a world's fair. The first two agenda items were money with which to build stuff and land on which to put the stuff. After scouring several areas of the city for large suitable plats of land, including Discovery Park and Sand Point, the World's Fair Study Commission decided on a relatively small chunk of land located just north of downtown, where the civic center was located. The opportunity to build structures that could be used after the event was an attractive proposition. After some wrangling, finagling, and fancy dancing, they acquired the seventy-four acres needed.

Now for the money. Although the average Seattleite didn't appear to have much civic interest in the event, Seattle voters approved a $7.5 million bond measure to help finance the fair by a stunning three-to-one margin. However, they'd need much more to mount such a monumental event. An initial attempt to get Olympia to loosen the state's purse strings failed, but after voters elected

Al Rossellini governor, the Washington State Legislature voted to match funds raised by Seattle.

It would still be tight, and they had much to build, but they found it helps to have powerful friends in high places. Warren G. Magnuson, an influential U.S. senator from Washington State, convinced Congress to appropriate $12.5 million for the fair. Next, the business community joined the act, donating funds. Seattle's largest employer, Boeing, actually had a policy prohibiting such promotions. So instead of donating money directly, they built the "Spacearium." The "Spacearium" was an interstellar simulator taking "passengers" on a sixty-quintillion-mile (eighteen zeros) trip through the stars at an unimaginable ten trillion times the speed of light. The fair folks, their wallets fat, moved on to the business of building. They hired some of the best people in their fields and said, "Build us a world-class fairground."

They hired architects to design the buildings, attractions, and landscapes, much of which remains to this day. Commissioner Eddie Carlson suggested an idea based on a TV tower with a revolving restaurant at the top he'd seen in Germany as the signature structure. This idea eventually became the Space Needle, Seattle's premier icon and one of the most recognizable structures on Earth. Other buildings included the Center House, the Coliseum, the Science Pavilion, the Opera House, the Mural Amphitheater, and the International "Singing" Fountain.

Heavy on a science and futuristic theme, fair organizers wanted a mode of transportation that would shout, "twenty-first century!" The result was the Seattle Center Monorail. The twin monorails would transport folks between the fairgrounds and Westlake Mall in downtown, a 1.2-mile trip gliding on magnetic rails in just over a minute and a half.

The fair finally opened with a flair, which included participation by President John F. Kennedy. President Kennedy, pressing the same golden nugget used to open the A-Y-P Exposition in 1909, activated a computer, which aimed a radio telescope at Cassiopeia A, a star approximately, and appropriately (remember Boeing's Spacearium), about sixty quintillion miles away. The radio telescope then received vibrations the star had emitted some ten thousand years ago, and scientists relayed them to Seattle, officially opening the 1962 World's Fair–Century 21 Exposition.

# JAVA MEN

## 1971

The siren whooped as the red and blue lights twinkled above the patrol car, splashing a light show against the dingy police parking garage walls.

"Where to first?" Derek asked his partner, Mike, as they prepared their police car for their tour of duty.

"Are you kidding me?" Mike began. "This is police work, young man; we have our priorities, remember?"

"Right. How could I have forgotten? I'm so ashamed." Derek lowered his head.

They stared, first at each other, and then straight ahead through the windshield. Derek shifted the car into gear and they said in unison, "To Starbucks!"

A tall, soft-spoken, dark-haired man in line ahead of the two officers had just placed his order. Both officers had immediately recognized him; only in Seattle could you find yourself in line at Starbucks behind the owner of that coffee empire, Howard Schultz.

"A short, nonfat latte, please," Derek asked.

Mike also placed his order, and all three men waited for their beverages while loitering near the barista's counter. The attractive barista smiled at her boss of bosses and announced the drink as she placed it on the shiny wood platform. Mr. Schultz began to reach but realized that it wasn't his drink that had been called, and he retracted his hand.

"Thank you," Derek said as the officer stepped forward and snatched up his cup.

Realizing that the barista had apparently confused whose order was whose, Mike looked at Derek and said, "Man, you better enjoy that coffee; it's gonna be the best cup you've ever had." Everyone chuckled and went about their business.

Now, just how did the Starbucks Coffee Company happen, and just how did it happen to change not only the currently coffee-saturated culture of Seattle and the greater Pacific Northwest but also of North America and much of the world?

Now, that's one long question, which deserves an even longer answer to do it justice. Some entrepreneurs create products or services that make our lives easier, happier, or just a little more interesting. However, it's truly rare to find a company that revolutionizes an industry and literally affects millions of people around the world. Starbucks is such a company.

Starbucks Coffee, Tea, and Spices was founded in 1971 with a small store in Seattle's Pike Place Public Market, very near where the "original" Starbucks store sits today. This is truly an American success story. One writer and two teachers, Gordon Bowker, Jerry Baldwin, and Zev Siegl, were up for a new business opportunity. They raised about $4,000 together and borrowed another five grand to finance a coffee shop, of which they literally built the structure themselves by investing their own sweat-equity—pounding nails and slapping paint on the walls.

For any fans of Herman Melville, the name the men chose for their business, *Starbucks,* isn't a mystery. It's the name of the java-craving first mate in Melville's classic novel *Moby Dick*—perfect. They designed an enchanting logo, the split-tailed siren, and voilà—the company was on its way to world dominance in the coffee-slinging biz.

Now, let's look at the creation of not only a corporate giant but also a bona fide worldwide phenomenon. You wouldn't be the first person to equate coffee with an illicit drug, and many a coffee aficionado refers to themselves as an "addict." You may have referred to yourself this way on occasion as well. (Not that you'd admit it, though.)

The men decided it best to build a firm foundation by committing to educating themselves about the coffee business, focusing on perfection, and conducting an aggressive marketing campaign. First, they looked to where the best in the business was brewing coffee magic. His name was Alfred Peet, and they found him brewing the beverage in Berkeley, California. Siegl spent six months attached to Peet's hip, learning the art of the coffee bean. One of the lessons that stuck was a commitment to excellence by choosing only the highest quality beans. Next was the marketing—and the natural correlation to the pushers of illicit "drugs"; the guys gave away tons of free coffee drinks with which to "hook" their clientele. Once hooked, they were customers for life. Many Seattleites can attest to the effectiveness of this particular marketing ploy.

It didn't take long before Starbucks became more autonomous. After buying beans from Peet for the better part of a year, in 1972 they invested in their own roaster and began roasting their own beans, giving them more control from bean to cup. They also opened their first location outside the Market, in Seattle's University Village shopping center.

By 1982 Starbucks was a local five-store chain, with locations in the Capitol Hill neighborhood, on University Way, and the first outside Seattle across the lake in the City of Bellevue. This was the state of the company when the aforementioned, and the most well-known of Starbucks owners, Howard Schultz came onboard as the company's retail sales and marketing manager.

It's interesting, and quite telling, that Schultz's interest in Starbucks coffee came after sampling the dark elixir and marveling at its superiority to the instant coffee he'd been accustomed to while growing up. Schultz was so struck by the product, he and his wife packed up and moved from New York to just about as far as you can get without leaving the continental United States: to Seattle. Ironically, at the time of this writing Starbucks Coffee is in the process of introducing its own instant coffee, Schultz having come full circle.

Following a coffee-culture immersion trip to Italy, Schultz returned to Seattle, inspired to re-create the ubiquitous coffee bars he'd visited there. However, Starbucks' owners weren't ready to abandon the wholesale coffee bean business and declined to implement Schultz's proposal. Schultz couldn't let go of the idea, so he left the company, but he did so under such good circumstances that his relationship with Starbucks remained strong, which would pay off down the line.

Schultz bought Peet's five coffee shops and renamed them Il Giornale. He served Starbucks coffee at these coffee bars. While Schultz's new enterprise was booming, the folks at Starbucks were running out of steam. Well, steam for coffee anyway. Bowker left the company to start some little project called Red Hook Ale—ever heard of it? However, Bowker didn't totally abandon his association with Starbucks: During the '90s Red Hook created Double-Black Stout, an exceeding dark brew containing Starbucks coffee.

Schultz, his eyes laser-focused on the future, offered the owners of Starbucks four million dollars for its six stores. They accepted the deal, Schultz renamed his existing stores, and the Starbucks Coffee empire was born.

# MURDERS MOST MACABRE

## 1983

A disheveled man in a torn gray coat and ill-fitting brown shoes drops an empty wine bottle and stumbles out of the recessed portico of a neglected building in Maynard Alley South, a narrow alleyway in the heart of Seattle's Chinatown. The steam from his breath rises into the lo-mien-tinged air. It's a doorway that invites all manner of vice activities and offers drunks a secluded nook in which to pass out for the night. The door is heavily chained and padlocked, but it doesn't matter; would-be intruders fear to trespass within its ghostly interior because of the dreadful crime committed here more than two and a half decades ago.

To find a business closed and the door shackled in an urban area is not particularly unusual, but to find a place held in such a solid state of abeyance for a quarter century *is* quite rare. February 19, 1983, was a rare Seattle day indeed. In fact, the horror that took place within the Wah Mee Club that night makes that date the rarest day of all the Emerald City's bad days. This is especially true for the victims' friends and family members, who find themselves haunted to this day by the worst mass murder in Seattle's history and by the decades-long, dragging court proceedings, which have left many in the community disappointed, to say the least.

On that cool midwinter morning, two men, one cocky, one anxious, arrived at the recessed alley entrance to a popular gambling establishment, the Wah Mee Club in Seattle's Chinatown. The Wah Mee had been a magnet for high-stakes gamblers for over fifty years. Armed with evil intent, a heinous plan, and the deadly weapons with which to carry it out, twenty-two-year-old Willie Mak, along with his partner Tony Ng, twenty-six years old, surveyed the alley and its surroundings before pressing the club's door buzzer. The man working security recognized both men and opened the door without hesitation.

Streams of smoke curled up into a blue-gray haze that drifted throughout the hall as the two strolled in among the gamblers. Mak was extremely agitated because his primary associate, twenty-year-old Benjamin Ng, hadn't yet arrived. Tony Ng (no relation to Benjamin), sweating more profusely than the temperature warranted, meandered to a seat, avoiding eye contact with the patrons.

Tony knew he shouldn't be there, but he feared Mak. Tony had initially agreed to accompany Mak in his plan to rob the Wah Mee's patrons because he owed Mak money. Tony had reportedly attempted to back out, instead offering to pay off his debt to Mak with money he'd borrowed from his girlfriend. Not wanting to risk another search for an additional accomplice, Mak threatened to kill Tony and members of Tony's family if he refused to assist in the crime. It wasn't fully accepted that Tony hadn't known that Mak had concocted such a coldly evil plan, which included killing everyone found within the Wah Mee Club that night because the gamblers would know the identities of the men who committed the robbery.

The alcohol flowed as freely as the money within the venerable old gambling den. A financial alchemy was in effect: The games within the establishment were in that slow but steady process of transferring the net worth of the assembled high-stakes gamblers into the net worth of the proprietors of the Wah Mee Club. The murmur was low and even, with only the slight, occasional nervous laughter coming from the mostly serious gamblers. Mak had estimated a haul from one to two hundred grand was possible.

A man with kind eyes and a soft smile slouched comfortably at a table, enjoying his meal. Tony Ng, his eyes darting about the room without landing, sat down next to the man. The man offered to share his food with Ng, who declined the offer. The old man didn't know it then, but he'd just offered to share his meal with a man who was about to help murder him.

Mak and Tony were waiting for Benjamin in order to put Mak's deadly plan into action. Benjamin had been tasked with bringing nylon cord with which to bind their victims. Mak, a man whose blood ran like ice crystals in his veins, had initially recruited Benjamin because of his long criminal history, particularly enamored that some of his offenses involved firearms.

Benjamin finally showed up just after midnight. With him he carried a bag containing several nylon cords cut to a predetermined length. The security guard recognized the man and immediately buzzed him into the club. Once Benjamin had entered the establishment, Mak wasted no time putting his plan into action. He nodded to Benjamin, who yelled for the six or seven patrons to get their hands up.

Stunned, the patrons raised their hands. The men held the security guard at gunpoint and forced him to allow additional victims into the club. Pointing guns at their heads, Mak and Benjamin then ordered their victims to the floor. Benjamin removed the nylon cords and the men began binding the captives' hands and feet, leaving them helpless, squirming on the floor. The men fished money and items from their victims' pockets. The security guard continued to admit patrons under duress, and each was shocked as they encountered the bound victims lying on the floor and were then also ordered to the floor at gunpoint, bound, and then robbed. By this time, the number of victims had doubled, and they may have felt a slight relief that they were still alive and the criminals' only intent was to rob them and then flee with their loot.

This feeling would have been short-lived; after the men had stuffed a bag full of thousands of dollars, Mak and Tony, in point-blank fashion, methodically fired bullets into the heads of their victims one after another. Blood streamed from gaping wounds and pooled on the floor surrounding the victims. The men continued until they'd expended all of their ammunition, and the people on the floor no longer screamed, moaned, or moved.

When the gunshots had subsided, only the jukebox played on, a surreal soundtrack behind an unspeakable crime. The pungent sulfur odor of burnt gunpowder blended into the already acrid, smoky atmosphere. Mak and his accomplices, satisfied each victim was dead, fled the Wah Mee in a small red car. On the way out of town they tossed their guns over the side of the I-90 floating bridge.

Willie Mak and Benjamin Ng were captured within hours of their murder spree. They hadn't counted on sixty-two-year-old Wai Chin surviving the carnage, escaping to get help, and informing the police that Mak and the two Ngs had committed the robberies and murders.

Meanwhile, Tony Ng had managed to escape to Canada, where he was located about eighteen months after the crime and arrested in Calgary's Chinatown in Alberta, Canada, and then extradited to the United States. Tony would not face the death penalty due to

Canada's conditions for extradition; instead he would face a life sentence if convicted of the slayings.

However, Tony was acquitted on the murder charges due to the claims of duress involved in his participation. Instead he was convicted of robbery and given multiple life sentences to be served concurrently. Benjamin Ng was convicted of the robberies and murders and received a life sentence for his crimes.

Mak's experience with the courts would be less straightforward than his compatriots'. His case meandered through the state and federal justice systems for almost twenty years, finally coming to a conclusion in 2002. He was initially sentenced to death in 1983, but after nearly two decades of wrangling in various courts, and much to the consternation of victims' family members, the U.S. Ninth Circuit Court of Appeals refused to reinstate Mak's death sentence. Instead, Mak will spend the rest of his days in prison for taking the lives of thirteen people and nearly killing one other on that chilly Chinatown night.

# GOODWILL RUNNING

## 1990

Jody's sweat-soaked, begging-for-mercy legs continued in motion, one stride following the other in a hypnotic cadence. As Jody trudged up the relatively mild incline at the south end of the Ballard Bridge, which now felt like Everest, people in pleasure boats cruising beneath yelled encouragement to the harriers braving the humid, merciless, ninety-degree, sun-baked course. Jody felt as if she were being tugged from behind by some mysterious force while similar forces pushed her from the front and pressed down on her from above. *Gravity's a bitch!*

*Why don't you just stop? It's okay; no one would think less of you*, she thought to herself. *You've gone seventeen miles, that's pretty close to the twenty-six point two.* Self-justification was having little effect.

In the grip of a fatigue-induced delirium, Jody gritted her teeth as she mused about the elite athletes competing in the event, most of whom had already finished the Goodwill Games Marathon and were probably poolside at this very moment relaxing with an umbrella drink at downtown Seattle's Olympic Four Seasons.

"I'll be out here twice as long as they were," she muttered. "And they have the nerve to call themselves *endurance* athletes." She smirked at the irony, shook her head, and trotted on.

Once across the bridge Jody hooked a right and headed toward Fremont with the final goal of Husky Stadium at the University of Washington steady in her mind's eye. One foot continued to reluctantly follow the other as if they were encrusted in concrete and she were running in thick mud. Some minor deliverance from the heat arrived in the form of homeowners standing in their front yards with garden hoses, spraying the passing runners with cool water.

Having completed a majority of the course, with the most challenging parts behind her, having crossed under Interstate 5 and now passing the University Hospital, she truly believed she was about to attain her goal. The finish line was now in view, and she was confident she'd cross it for sure, but only after running the longest one hundred yards she'd ever run in her life.

Jody wobbled into the recovery tent in the Husky Stadium parking lot on all but spent legs. Her legs trembled, and she fought to remain upright as she snatched up food and drink from the snack tables. Her husband and children ran up to congratulate her, her kids wrapping arms around their hero's legs, nearly knocking her over. She barely managed the strength to return their hugs. Jody had just completed the most difficult athletic test of her life. She'd just competed, officially, in the "citizens" category of the 1990 Seattle Goodwill Games.

Enigmatic master entrepreneur Ted Turner created the Goodwill Games in 1985. The games were established to counteract the negativity drawn toward international amateur sports resulting from the reciprocally boycotted Olympic Games of 1980 (Los Angeles) and 1984 (Moscow). The first Goodwill Games was held in Moscow in 1986, and even before those games commenced, a Seattle Organizing

Committee was established to vie to become the first U.S. city to host the games. In June 1986 Ted Turner announced he'd selected Seattle as the site of the 1990 Goodwill Games.

The 1990 Seattle Goodwill Games, although not the Olympics, were planned to attract the best athletes from around the world, therefore setting the stage for a vast local and international audience. Instead of each nation selecting the athletes who would compete, the respective athletic federations of the various sports made the selections.

The Seattle games would host some 2,300 athletes from over fifty nations who would compete in twenty-one sports, including such diverse events as swimming (traditionally summer) and hockey (traditionally winter). The Soviet Union would be making its inaugural appearance in the sport of baseball. Some of the more famous athletes to take part in the 1990 Seattle games were Carl Lewis, Leroy Burrell, Ian Thorpe, Marion Jones, Oscar de la Hoya, Oksana Baiul, and Jackie Joyner-Kersee.

There were a few elements that set the Goodwill Games apart from other international athletic events. One of those elements was two additional, nonathletic appendages to the games. One was an arts festival, and the other was a business conference. This added a new dimension, which helped to bring nations together as the world was changing, in fact, rapidly headed toward the collapse of the Soviet Bloc.

Still, one of the most unique elements of these games, and an aspect that truly distinguished the Goodwill Games from the Olympic Games, was the inclusion in the Goodwill Games Marathon of a "citizen" category. This event allowed the average person the possibility of more than a mere visceral participation in the games. Jody, and other average—and true amateur—runners, could officially participate in this international athletic competition.

Whether these specific games were considered a success (the Goodwill Games having since gone defunct) is arguable depending on one's perspective. However, as the old saying goes: nothing ventured; nothing gained. And Ted Turner did indeed undertake a venture that provided many athletes, artists, business-folk, and ordinary citizens with the opportunity to compete with or meet some of the best athletes, artisans, and businesspeople the world had to offer.

Slumped on a folding chair, Jody felt the cold metal providing a measure of relief for her overheated body. Her three small children, not understanding the physical and mental impact such an exertion had on their mother, asked all manner of questions. "Are you tired, Mommy?" "Was it far, Mommy?" "Can we go for ice cream now, Mommy?" Jody perked up at the last question; that sounded like a great idea.

After a trip to the ice-cream shop, Jody managed to coax her legs into transporting her a few hundred more yards across the street, to the shores of Green Lake, where she dangled her spent feet in the water, lay back on a bright beach towel, and no doubt fell into a deep, well-earned afternoon nap, but hopefully not to dream of being back out on the course, with thousands of other runners from around the world, of the most exciting athletic event in which she'd ever competed.

# THE INCREDIBLE SINKING BRIDGE

1990

"Man, when's this rain gonna stop?" Bryan plucked a banana out of his lunchbox and began peeling it. Bob, shaking his head, poured a cup of black coffee out of his thermos for himself and Brandon. "Don't ask me; my garage has been flooding like you wouldn't believe."

"You too? I had to dig trenches to route the water away from my foundation," Bryan said.

Brandon smiled knowingly. "Hey, that's exactly what I had to do. Well, I knew Seattle was rainy when I moved here, but this is ridiculous."

The three men tucked under a blue tarp they'd strung across some machinery on the deck of the Lacey V. Murrow Memorial Bridge, more commonly known as the Lake Washington, or I-90, Floating Bridge. The work wasn't normally bad—operating hydro-demolition machinery was great work in good or even just wet weather—but add a sharp wind to the equation and pleasure was not an apt adjective associated with the job.

Hydro-demolition is a process that employs high-pressure water jets rather than the destructive vibrations of jackhammers to remove concrete. This type of machinery is best used for jobs where concrete must be removed, but the majority of the structure's integrity must be retained. Their task was to remove sidewalks in order to widen the bridge as a part of its refurbishing.

The storm whipped up the waves, sending stinging spray into the men's faces. The men recoiled from the beating weather when they suddenly heard a strange sound that rose above the roar of the wind and water.

"What the hell was that?" Bryan looked around and then back at Bob and Brandon. Bob, who'd been sitting on a plastic bucket, stood. "I don't know; never heard that before."

Then the three men listed sideways, nearly losing their balance. The entire bridge had shifted. "Holy crap!" Brandon yelled. "I think this thing's going down."

"The bridge?" Bob asked.

"What else?" Bryan said.

The bridge shifted again, and the loud screech of twisting concrete and metal creased the air.

"Go for the tug," Bryan shouted, pointing to the tugboat tied up near their end of the bridge deck. Bryan and Bob started toward it, but Brandon stepped in the opposite direction. A momentary pause in the bridge's structural crisis had given Brandon the illusion of more time.

"Where the hell you going?" Bryan and Bob yelled in unison.

"Getting my lunchbox; I'm not leaving without my thermos— I've had it forever," Brandon said.

"You dork! Get over here or you'll be drinking from your thermos permanently at the bottom of the lake," Bryan said.

"I'll be right th—" Brandon began when the bridge deck shifted in earnest, and horrendous, hissing air bursts from busting submerged compartments surrounded the men. Brandon had an apparent and immediate change of heart. He dashed toward Bryan and Bob, catching up to and passing them en route to the tug. Some members of the tug crew helped the men aboard while another untied the boat from its mooring on the bridge.

"I don't think anyone in their wildest dreams thought this would happen," said Police Chief Patrick Fitzsimons during an impromptu press conference called in response to the sinking of the 6,620-foot floating bridge in November of 1990. The comment aptly summarized the shock the Seattle area community felt when a 2,800-foot chunk of the bridge that had been carrying them across Lake Washington for fifty years suddenly twisted, pulled away, and sank, and was now resting at the bottom of Lake Washington.

When most bridges fail, folks report that the bridge had collapsed. However, in the case of the I-90 Bridge, it's what's called a pontoon bridge, which is built much like a large marine vessel. It's comprised of a series of watertight compartments to provide buoyancy, allowing the bridge to float. When the bridge was opened, it was the longest floating bridge in the world at the time. It's currently the second longest next to its sister to the north, the Evergreen Point Floating Bridge.

The bridge was originally opened in 1940 with toll booths installed to pay for its construction. (Incidentally, these toll booths remain in service as area latte carts.) Naysayers complained the bridge would never work, disbelieving that a structure so large and built of concrete could stay afloat let alone transport an estimated two thousand vehicles a day across the lake. Not only did it float and carry those vehicles, it actually carried up to five thousand vehicles per day, and that number soared ever higher after the tolls were removed in 1946.

Now, this story is an object lesson in good intentions and unintended consequences, since over the past four decades or so, those purporting to support the environment apparently created a situation that, while attempting to avoid polluting Lake Washington, actually resulted in contaminating the lake by a thousandfold.

The concrete wash residue created by the hydro-demolition was considered contaminated under the applicable environmental laws and therefore couldn't be sloughed into the lake. The engineers determined that the separate pontoons or compartments could be used to store the "contaminants," rather than dumping the concrete and water mixture. So, in order to complete this function, workers had to remove the watertight doors from the pontoons and then fill the spaces with the deposits.

Unfortunately, this created a conspiracy of circumstances that spelled doom for the floating bridge. With the doors removed, with the pontoons filled with concrete residue, and with the addition of heavy rains and seeping lake water, only catastrophe could result.

Fortunately, no one was killed when the bridge sank. The bridge gave plenty of warning that it was about to give up its career as a floating bridge for one as a sunken bridge. Additionally, this bridge was being refurbished in order to remain in service to augment the new bridge that was built to its immediate south. As the bridge capsized and submerged, it damaged several cables stabilizing the new bridge. This caused construction officials to close the new bridge while divers inspected it for damage, but it was soon open to traffic once again.

This collapse served to provide an education in construction's, and more to this point, demolition's, unintended consequences. In the future it will serve as a lesson to aspiring engineers working with floating bridge technologies, which will hopefully allow them to prevent any such similar catastrophes.

# THE SEATTLE SOUND

## 1990

On October 4, 1992, a reasonably orderly mass of faded, tattered-clothed Seattle music fans stood in line on a downtown sidewalk waiting to flood into the Crocodile Café to enjoy a performance by pioneering "grunge" band Mudhoney. The flannel-shirted faithful outside the "Croc" were about to learn the three bucks they'd paid for the specially priced tickets was one of the best investments they'd ever made, or probably would ever make, in their music-loving lives.

Billed as Mudhoney's opening act for the evening's concert was a mystery band (and this in a town where music aficionados knew *all* the good bands) named Pen Cap Chew. The fans filed into the snug, or shall we say intimate, environs of the Croc. Some of the more hyped-up fans immediately began winding up the frenzy in the mosh pit, arms and legs flailing, bodies colliding, warming up for the show. However, the moshers' slam-dancing fury slowed and then suddenly froze. The fans were held in stunned abeyance as they began to catch glimpses of the opening act's band members.

As Pen Cap Chew took the stage, the dazed concertgoers stood in shocked silence before a band that bore a striking resemblance to the most popular band in the world at that time, Nirvana—it was Nirvana! And *Nirvana* described a musical version of exactly where the fans were spiritually transported to as they realized their outrageous good fortune.

The Croc was arguably the preeminent grunge music venue in Seattle, hosting all of the biggies of the "Seattle Sound," as well as other rock, blues, and punk artists, over its sixteen-year run. Unfortunately, and quite surprisingly, the Croc shut its doors suddenly in 2007. The venue fit with so-called grunge's beginnings: It was relatively small and unassuming but accommodating—friendly.

On October 10, 1998, the promoters at the Croc pulled another rabbit out of that hat with a surprise opening act for one of the 1970s biggies, Cheap Trick. Another shocked crowd was again surprised into stunned silence the night Pearl Jam took to the stage. The Croc was so deep into the Seattle music scene, it's been included in the lyrics of songs and has at least twice been a setting for scenes in movies, including the 1992 Seattle grunge movie *Singles* (starring Matt Dillon, Bridget Fonda, Kyra Sedgwick, and Tom Skerrit). *Singles* was a moderately popular release, but its soundtrack went platinum and was one of the best-selling motion picture soundtracks of the 1990s. In fact, it's been credited with helping to fuel the Seattle music scene's (grunge) initial conflagration and eventual explosion onto the world music landscape.

So grunge-tinged was the movie *Singles* that a plethora of princes of the genre appeared in the movie. Alice in Chains, Pearl Jam, and Soundgarden excellently provided authentic flavor to the background and sound of the movie. Various individual band members also appeared, some in speaking roles: Eddie Vedder, Chris Cornell, Stone Gossard, and Jeff Ament, to name but a few.

Although this chapter heading indicates 1990 as the date for the birth of grunge, its actual roots go back to the mid-'80s. However, for our purposes, 1990 seems to be—okay, arguably—the year in which grunge began to get traction in the entertainment mainstream.

Any mass music movement comprises at least three major components that support it: quality artists, passionate fans, and competent promoters. Without any one of these legs, the movement is likely to collapse. The entertainment annals are replete with stories of the "ten-year" overnight success. Seattle's grunge music explosion is no exception. Many Seattle musicians, including those mentioned above, have associations with one or more of the various bands that were involved in the grunge phenomenon. Band members moved into, out of, and through many of them.

For example, Jeff Ament and Stone Gossard were integral members of Mother Love Bone before the band's able voice, Andrew Wood, died, after which the two went on to help form the rock phenomenon Pearl Jam. The story of the birth and growth of Seattle's grunge involves remarkable bands, fans, promoters, and venues.

The grunge volcano didn't erupt until folks like Kurt Cobain and Nirvana, Eddie Vedder and Pearl Jam, Chris Cornell and Soundgarden, and Jerry Cantrell and Alice in Chains hit the scene in 1991. And although '91 has been credited as the year Grunge Music, or Seattle Rock was born, there were bands that preceded these giants, laying much of the groundwork, inciting an eager audience of antsy, angst-filled youth, and providing much inspiration.

Two of the bands credited with fabricating a foundation for what would come to be known as grunge for others to follow were the Melvins, which formed in 1985, and Mudhoney, which formed in 1988. These bands didn't just provide inspiration to other Seattle artists; in the case of Kurt Cobain, they provided him with a job as a roadie and they groomed him as their protégé. Of course Kurt went on to rise above all the booming Seattle personalities and bands, and accrued some clout within the music industry. The relationship formed between Kurt and the Melvins would later pay off for the band when, endorsed by Cobain, they signed with a major label.

The bands that formed early on in the '80s were influenced by several genres and subgenres that had evolved out of the '60s, '70s, and '80s, such as the deep bass, hard guitar, and big drum sounds of Black Sabbath and Deep Purple, along with the energy and rage of punk acts like the Sex Pistols, and the dramatic showmanship of blues-inspired hard rock bands such as Aerosmith.

When watching these bands perform, one can see all of these elements are present either subtly or overtly. For fans who weren't able to enjoy these performers live as they forged a new genre, they could see it plainly in MTV music video performances like Pearl Jam's "Even Flow" taped at the Moore Theater in Seattle, and Nirvana's "Smells Like Teen Spirit." The hard-driving guitar, bass, and drums raked like long fingernails across an itchy back, soothing the fans who desperately needed to be scratched.

Whether you grew up along with the grunge movement from its 1980s birth in the cluttered garages and small clubs in and around Seattle, or you were swept up and tossed and turned in the grungy tsunami of the 1990s, there aren't many who escaped its influence. Grunge still remains popular today and continues as an influence on music and the popular culture.

# THE DAY THE MUSIC DIED—AGAIN

## 1994

A long-haired young man wearing baggy, threadbare blue jeans cut off just below the knees, a green T-shirt shrouded by a dingy, red tartan flannel shirt, and heavy black boots shuffles along the winding sidewalk in the 100 block of Lake Washington Boulevard East, a neighborhood located along the affluent shores of Seattle's Lake Washington between the Madrona and Madison Park neighborhoods. He's holding hands with a pretty, spiky-haired blonde girl, her face pierced with jewelry in several places. Similarly attired, she has a black denim backpack slung over her shoulder. He's holding a folded scrap of white paper in his free hand, intermittently looking up from it and glancing around the neighborhood, appearing perplexed.

They stop and approach a couple of landscapers trimming hedges surrounding an opulent Spanish-accented house. The landscapers point to a modest-size patch of green about a hundred yards north before the young pilgrims even speak a word. The couple smile broadly and nod to the workmen as they resume their pace. Their eyes widen; their mouths are agape; they are so near their goal they can almost taste it.

Suddenly the pair freeze in place, jaws hung low; they both unconsciously raise their hands to their faces. Reverent expressions conveying both awe and sadness dominate their faces. They'd seen the place in pictures in magazines, but now they are actually here, in front of *his* house. They stand mesmerized, staring at a large gray home surrounded by a low wall of brick and a high wall of thick green rhododendron. Access to the property is controlled by a sturdy wooden security gate.

Immediately to the south of the hallowed house is a verdant two-acre parcel named Viretta Park. The two tread in somber contemplation over to a lone bench located near the center of the park in the shadows of towering conifers. They glance at the graffiti, inscribed names, and tributes scarring its surface. The two stroll the grounds and then stop and stare at the empty space where once stood a garage with a room above, adjacent the main home. In this room was where "the music" died—*again,* some fifteen years ago (joining Buddy Holly, Jimi Hendrix, Elvis, etc.). The two then return to the bench, sit at opposite ends, and then set to etching their own contributions to the crude but sincere memorial.

This oft-repeated scene may best describe the impact that a twenty-seven-year-old musician named Kurt Donald Cobain, lead singer of the most popular band on earth at the time of his death, Nirvana, had on the music world. These pilgrimages are a phenomenon that continues fifteen years after the death of one of grunge music's princes, and one that shows no hint of subsiding.

Music hooked Cobain early in his life, his first guitar a gift when he turned fourteen years old. However, he never fell in love with the soul-searing, brilliant light of fame that would accompany his love of music. This dichotomy would haunt him for most of his professional career. In a world where so many musicians of little, modest, or adequate talent strive for fame and fortune, Cobain was a young man of elevated talent who strived to produce his music while attempting to evade that intrusive, invasive public microscope.

Cobain, along with Krist Novoselic, formed Nirvana in 1986 and together with various drummers performed at a variety of venues around the northwest and produced their first album, *Bleach,* in 1989. In 1991 fortune began to percolate for the band when they finally found a perfect fit behind the drums in the form of the talented and affable Dave Grohl, currently of Foo Fighters fame, a band he formed in 1995. Percolation transitioned to full frenetic boil after the release of the mega-massive, multi-everything hit album *Nevermind.* Tunes like "Smells Like Teen Spirit," "Come As You Are," and "Lithium" rocked and rolled the rock 'n' roll world.

Ironically it was Cobain's destiny to succeed professionally that may have set him up to fail personally and which has often had more than one fan likely reassessing the meaning of success and failure. As is the case with so many artists who die young, either accidentally or by their own hand, substance abuse is often the means, or at least a contributing component, leading to the person's demise—Kurt Cobain was no different.

Cobain suffered a miserable series of drug abuse-related incidents, some of which resulted in grave medical conditions and others of which led to admittance into various recovery and rehabilitation facilities. Considering his eventual demise, it's apparent that none of these helped much.

Cobain married Courtney Love in 1992 and by many accounts didn't find the contentment he may have been seeking through the marriage. However, one indubitable blessing he enjoyed without reservations was the birth of his daughter, Frances Bean, in August of 1992. Frances was one of the few bright lights in Cobain's life, which he welcomed with his heart opened wide.

In 1993 the band released *In Utero.* Although the album was a success by any normal assessment, having followed such an abnormally earth-shattering smash as *Nevermind,* the expectations were so high that by comparison their record label was disappointed from a business perspective. Business insinuating itself into the creative process apparently helped to drive Cobain to hair-tearing frustration. Playing the huge stadiums and arenas were a necessary evil, with an emphasis on *evil,* especially for a man who preferred the intimate environs of the smaller venues, such as the Crocodile Café in downtown Seattle, in which he'd performed while coming up back in the late 1980s.

Nirvana taped a classic performance on MTV's *Unplugged* in November 1993, which was broadcast to raves that December and which became a number-one release about a year later, following Cobain's death. Nirvana next played a concert in Germany, after which Cobain again abused drugs and found himself in a hospital in serious condition. After minimal recovery, he left the hospital without notifying any family or friends. In early April 1994, Cobain disappeared; no one knew where he'd gone for several days.

The mystery of Cobain's whereabouts was solved by a workman who found the singer's body on April 8, 1994. Cobain had apparently returned to his home on the lake in Seattle. Sadly, while there, after scribbling his last words on a note, he retrieved his shotgun, placed the barrel to his head, and pulled the trigger. An influential voice of an anxious generation fell silent on April 5, 1994.

Despite aggressive conspiracy theorists expounding to the contrary, the King County Medical Examiner's Office ruled that Kurt Cobain had taken his own life by his own hand. The autopsy report indicated that no evidence existed that would point to the involvement of any other person or that the death had occurred due to any other cause.

Although Cobain's life ended tragically, his music has gone on to inspire the music generation he'd captured so effectively. Judging by current airplay, Kurt Cobain's influence through Nirvana's songs will continue to stir generations of music lovers for many years to come.

# FOUR HEROES GAVE THEIR ALL

## 1995

The mood surrounding the property was as somber as any gray Seattle day. It was January 5, 1995. Heavy equipment worked carefully alongside workers within the rubble of a large Chinatown warehouse, which had contained a frozen-food business, a rock band rehearsal stage, and a storage space. The stench of burnt lumber mixed with the diesel fuel of the tractors permeated the crisp winter air. Suddenly the work came to a standstill as someone called out that the body of another of the four firefighters killed in the fire had been located.

Four Seattle firefighters retrieved their fallen comrade, reverently placed their brother's charred remains on a gurney, covered his body, and carried him to a waiting Seattle Fire Department (SFD) Aid Car. The firefighters and police officers on-site snapped to attention and saluted the fallen hero as his body passed them. Similarly, eight Seattle Police Department (SPD) motorcycle officers stood in a rigid line, crisply saluting, honoring the firefighter as he was placed into the rig. They slammed the doors shut, flashing red lights burst overhead, and the vehicle rolled solemnly from the scene. The solo units mounted their police motorcycles and flowed to a position in front of the aid car, providing a rolling honor-guard escort to the King County Medical Examiner's Office a short distance away.

The conflagration that has come to be known as the Pang Warehouse Fire shocked the city and deeply wounded the men and women of the SFD, long considered one of America's elite fire departments. How could such a tragedy have happened to such a competent fire department, which had only a half decade earlier, on September 9, 1989, suffered the loss of SFD Lieutenant Matthew Johnson in the Blackstock Lumber Fire? The department had implemented enhanced safety policies, equipment, and tactics, which had increased the safety of Seattle's firefighters. At least that was the belief, but even the best of departments can suffer from a conspiracy of circumstances, which can cause a tragedy that exceeds the effect of each individual element.

Several factors conspired over the eighty-five-year history of the primarily wooden structure, which housed the Mary Pang Food Warehouse in Seattle's Chinatown. One was a raising of the surface grade, or street level, which essentially turned a former ground-level floor into a "hidden" basement. It was in this hidden basement that a "pony wall" of insufficient integrity to support the floor above had been built at some indeterminate time in the past. (A "pony wall" is a new wall attached to and extending an existing wall.) And although the SFD had made some significant progress in firefighter safety since the Blackstock fire of 1989, in which tactical deficiencies were partly responsible for Lt. Johnson's death and had since been corrected, something had obviously failed at the Pang Warehouse that fateful day.

However, there is one factor that rises above all others when considering the cause of the fire and the resulting deaths of four firefighters. The primary blame belongs to a man with a match and a motive named Martin Pang. Martin Pang is the adopted son of Mary and Harry Pang—Mary, the sister of Seattle legend Ruby Chow, and Harry, a WWII B-17 gunner and decorated hero. The Pangs were the proprietors of a successful Chinese frozen-foods business, which was housed in this warehouse located in a semi-industrial area at the edge of Chinatown at Maynard Avenue South and South Dearborn Street.

Martin Pang had worked for his parents in the frozen-foods business, but at the time of the crime he was living in southern California and working toward an acting career. However, he had other more nefarious ideas about "re-involving" himself in the business. Pang made plans to destroy his parents' warehouse by setting the building ablaze. He hoped to benefit from the insurance payout and through the financial gains a property cleared for new development would bring.

Pang started the blaze in the lowest portion of the building, which had essentially become a hidden basement with only a "pony wall" supporting the floor above it. The view from the exterior gave no indication that a level existed below what was thought to be the ground floor. A musician arriving for band practice discovered the fire at around 7:00 p.m. and called the fire department.

SFD incident commanders formulated an attack plan and deployed fire units to areas of responsibility surrounding the L-shaped building. The fire began as a one-alarm call-out, but before the night was over it would grow to five alarms with over one hundred firefighters battling the deadly inferno.

Unknown to the vast majority of fire personnel on scene, some of the SFD hierarchy were advised that this warehouse was a possible arson target. In fact, surveillance had been set up on the building but was discontinued more than two weeks prior to the fire. The lack of dissemination of this information may or may not have had an effect on how the fire was approached, but SFD learned that a little information is better than no information in all fires.

Another problem was there were no "pre-fire" building plans available to the officers and firefighters attacking the flames. Again, investigators would later determine that due to the age and nature of the old building, even if fire personnel had inspected the basement of the building, unless they were construction experts and knew what they were looking for, they probably wouldn't have determined any obvious problems with the "pony wall" in the space.

Regardless, knowing there was a basement room at all would have been crucial information in this case. The firefighters battling the interior fire found themselves in dark smoke with no flames, and a bit confused as to where exactly the fire was. Unfortunately, unknown to the firefighters, the fire was burning beneath their feet, compromising the integrity of the "pony wall" supporting them as each moment passed.

Finally the floor shifted before giving way and collapsing like a single-hinged trapdoor, sending two firefighters to their immediate deaths, their bodies later recovered where they'd fallen. Two other firefighters fell into the fiery abyss, but apparently they survived the initial fall and attempted to escape, as they were found yards away from where they'd fallen through the floor.

Twenty-two-year veteran Lt. G. M. Shoemaker, forty-three; twenty-four-year veteran Lt. W. D. Kilgore, forty-five; four-year firefighter R. R. Terlicker, thirty-five; and J. T. Brown, twenty-five, with only three years on the department, were killed in the line of duty. Seven other firefighters were injured but survived their wounds.

Following the fire, Pang reportedly "returned" to Seattle to provide comfort to his distraught parents. However, as fingers began pointing Pang's way, he fled to Brazil, a country that would not extradite for murder or potential death penalty cases. After significant pressure from the U.S. government, and after holding Pang for a year in a Brazilian jail, that country agreed to extradite Pang to the United States, but only if charges were amended to manslaughter. Pang would eventually plea bargain and receive a thirty-five-year sentence, avoiding a possible life sentence for arson.

The fallout from the case resulted in the lost firefighters' families filing lawsuits against the fire department. These cases resulted in jury awards to victims' families ranging between $450,000 and $5.6 million. Also following from the tragic deaths, the fire department was fined for several violations, including ignoring the department's safety chief, who'd recommended the implementation of safety policies that could have mitigated this tragedy. These sanctions led to many improvements in SFD's fire safety policies and practices. Firefighters were issued "Nomex" hoods to prevent burns to neck and ears, and they acquired thermal-imaging cameras capable of "seeing in the dark." SFD now maintains a database of building plans, and the department formed special rescue teams to respond to multi-alarm fires.

In Seattle's Pioneer Square today, not far from where this catastrophe occurred, a statue stands where folks can pay their respects to the four heroes who fell that January day in 1995, and to those twenty-seven heroes who've sacrificed their lives for the community they serve since 1891.

# BUS PLUNGES OFF BRIDGE

## 1998

The coach hissed to a stop, punctuated by a loud squeal from the brakes. A frumpy Indian woman wearing a tattered red coat and a green and yellow trucker's cap worn over a red bandana flipped a bus transfer toward the bus driver, who barely acknowledged her boarding. She sniffed, stuffed the scrap back into her pocket, and shuffled down the sticky aisle, slightly losing her balance as the coach lurched forward before she found a seat. Regaining her footing, she worked her way to a side-facing seat toward the rear of the bus, dropped her bundles, and slid into the seat.

It wasn't that late in the evening, but it was already getting dark as the year drew nearer the solstice. A stoic man was sitting a couple of seats away from her; all the other passengers were seated well ahead of them toward the front half of the bus. She could tell the man was tall even though he was sitting; his legs sprouted awkwardly from his body. The man wore sunglasses, despite it being nearly dark outside.

The man shifted in his seat and looked at the woman but glanced away when she peeked his way and caught his eye. As he looked back, she'd maintained her gaze. The man slid closer to the woman. She didn't move away, her mouth creased into a subtle smile, she nodded. After a bit of small talk, the man placed his hand inside his jacket and sighed deeply.

Slowly, he withdrew his hand from his jacket pocket. "You see this?" He was holding a handgun. He glanced up toward the front of the bus. No passengers looked in his direction. The woman nodded, her eyes shifting about, but she remained calm, although concern wrinkled her face.

"What's that for?" she asked.

"It's a shame how people behave on the bus." He raised his chin toward two young black men poking at each other playfully, barely a minor nuisance to most folks but obviously disturbing to the mysterious dark-spectacled passenger.

The woman shrugged.

"And those drivers. . . ." The man shook his head slowly and turned toward the front of the bus as his eyes narrowed and hardened, riveted on the back of the bus driver's head. "Why are some of 'em so mean?"

The woman shrugged again and said, "Not much you can do."

The man turned back to her for a moment and then scanned the coach as if counting the number of passengers. He turned back to the woman. "I'm gonna get another gun."

Steven Gary Cool, aka Silas Cool, forty-three, got off the bus and strolled off into the night, his sunglasses still firmly wrapping his face. He was intent on keeping his promise to get another gun. The woman on the bus to whom he'd shown his gun and had foreshadowed his violence did not tell the police what she'd seen and heard from Silas—until *afterward*.

On November 27, 1998, Cool boarded another Metro Coach, but this time, rather than simple frustration, he'd carried aboard with him a sinister plan. No one knows the precise carnage Cool had in mind for the bus driver and his passengers, but it's not out of the realm of conjecture to assume he'd intended the worst—the death of every single person aboard.

Cool sat patiently awaiting the right moment. With the bus approaching the Aurora Bridge, that moment had arrived. He rose from his seat and strode deliberately toward the front of the coach, his steel eyes locked on his prey. When he arrived behind the driver, McLaughlin, Cool withdrew his gun and quickly fired two shots into McLaughlin's body, sending the passengers into a panic and the large bus careening out of control as it drove onto the beginning portion of the bridge, which carried traffic over a residential area. Cool then raised the gun to his own head and pulled the trigger, sending a bullet through his brain, ending his life, but not the nightmare he'd set into motion for the other passengers, and for those innocent people below.

Due primarily to the courageous actions of mortally wounded Metro Transit driver Mark McLaughlin, aside from Cool and McLaughlin, all but one of the passengers survived the horrendous crash. Sadly, sixty-nine–year-old Herman Liebelt was killed in the crash.

Investigators later determined the bus was traveling at forty-nine miles per hour, and at that speed the sixty-foot-long, twenty-ton coach would likely have smashed through the bridge rail and plunged into the icy waters of the ship canal below, probably killing all aboard. Instead, McLaughlin managed to apply the brakes enough to slow the coach by about ten miles per hour, causing the vehicle to hit the rail at a point before it was over the water and at a point much lower in height from which to fall to the ground.

When the coach went over the side of the bridge, it glanced off a two-story apartment building before slamming to the earth. Calls inundated Seattle's 911 police and fire systems. Multiple Seattle police and fire department units, as well as private ambulance services and civilians, responded to the mass casualty incident. The sight was surreal, but at the time those initially responding imagined the incident to be a tragic collision, not a murder/suicide and attempted mass murder.

To say Silas Cool was a troubled individual is to engage in understatement. As is always the case with such tragedies, once the pieces of the puzzle are put into place, prevention seems, if not obvious, at least apparent, if preventative actions had been available or even possible. Cool had come from a fairly well-to-do background: A family member had provided him with a $30,000 certificate of deposit, and his parents provided a sizable stipend for their son's expenses. Despite this largesse available to him, he was known to take his meals at soup kitchens and obtain his groceries at food banks.

Although Cool had not been seen by any mental health professionals and therefore had never been diagnosed with any mental disorder, the signs were reportedly apparent. Keeping in mind what they say about hindsight, he'd worked for the county government, where he was described as antisocial and racist. He also had a significant string of misdemeanor arrests, including obstructing, false reporting, theft, and once for being a "peeping Tom," all not unusual crimes for folks with mental issues who get into trouble with the law.

This heinous crime showed yet again the mental conditions and/or evil that can exist in or possess an individual. Unfortunately, such tragedies can occur anytime. However, it also points up another thing: the heroism of ordinary people. While the 911 dispatchers were topnotch, and the professional first-responders such as police officers, firefighters and paramedics, and ambulance techs did a stellar job, the stories of ordinary, average Seattleites responding to assist those injured in the crash were inspiring. Although a tragic incident indeed, without the heroic efforts of all involved, from the bus driver to the eager-to-help civilians, the incident could have been much, much worse.

# THE SECOND BATTLE OF SEATTLE

## 1999

"You ever hear this one?" the affable young man with brown hair pulled back into a frizzy ponytail asked the cops standing above him from his seated position on the damp asphalt of Pike Street. His arms were linked with two girls, one frumpy, one pretty, sandwiching him. The demonstrator was one link in a chain that was part of a sea of ten thousand or more demonstrators crammed into the intersection at Sixth Avenue and Pike Street. A skirmish line of approximately twenty-five riot-helmeted police officers spanned from the Sheraton Hotel's entrance across the street to the west.

The young man who'd posed the question wore a blue Nike shirt, a dingy white baseball cap (worn backward) with a New York Yankee's baseball emblem, and leather work boots, and he held a silver cell phone in his hand. He and the pretty blonde girl sitting to his left had been grilling the officers on their "shameless" participation in protecting the "corrupt" WTO, and regaled the officers with their unsolicited political views—and jokes. The frumpy girl seemed miffed at her compatriot's attempt at levity. For the most part, the officers avoided engaging the protesters in political conversation, which was the most prudent policy for many reasons.

"What one?" one of the officers finally replied, apparently willing to interact in what appeared to be an apolitical overture.

"Seems this guy goes to see a psychiatrist because he's been having trouble sleeping," the kid says. Other officers and other protesters turn toward the joke-teller.

"'Tell me what's the problem,' the doctor asked the man.

"'Well, last week I dreamed I had two wigwams and couldn't decide which one to sleep in. Then I woke up and couldn't get back to sleep.'

"'Okay; that was probably just temporary.'

"'Well, after dreaming about two wigwams last week, this week I dreamt about two tepees, and then I woke up and couldn't get back to sleep. What's wrong with me, Doc?'

"The doctor gazed thoughtfully at the ceiling, pursed his lips, and scratched his chin. Suddenly, he clapped his hands together and said, 'I've got it. I know what's wrong with you.'

"The doctor paused.

"'Well—?' the troubled man prompted him.

"'The problem is . . . you're too tense!'"

The officers and those in the crowd who'd been listening stood silent, the punch line sailing over their heads like a teargas grenade that lands and fails to explode—a dud.

The protester-jokester smiled. "Get it?" he asked. "The psychiatrist said the man was . . . [overly enunciated] TWO TENTS!"

Everyone broke into laughter; even the sterner cops rolled their eyes and snickered, all except for the blonde, who maintained a perplexed expression. He tapped her on the forehead and elaborated. "Two tents—Wigwams?—Tepees?"

The blonde girl rolled her eyes, "Oh geez," but she reluctantly joined in the laughter.

Just then, from across the intersection came a loud banging sound rising above the din of the crowd. Several young people dressed in ratty dark clothing, hoods up and faces covered with bandanas, carrying plump backpacks, were slamming wooden protest sign stakes and other items against the large windows of Nike Town. Finally, with the impacts increasing and the frenzy growing, the large glass window gave way, shattering jagged shards all over the sidewalk to the cheers of a significant portion of the demonstrators, but to the consternation of the majority. The immense size of the crowd prevented police from making any arrests in the incident.

This bipolar vignette was just a miniscule slice of the action that took place over the week that saw a naive Seattle come of age in the worst riots in the city's history, but it also demonstrates the yin and yang of that tumultuous week. To say that Seattle officials were ill-prepared for the WTO conferences is not an opinion, but as settled history as any event can be. By all accounts city officials' expectations and initial security plans were at best incorrect, at worst incompetent.

*Surreal.* This was the word most used by all groups involved to describe normally mellow Seattle during the WTO demonstrations. A strange mélange of people flocked to the area and then swarmed into downtown Seattle, cramming into the streets surrounding the Washington State Convention Center: Union workers, anarchists, socialists, communists; delegates, political officials, businesspeople, security details; cops from law enforcement agencies all over the state; and soldiers from the Washington Army National Guard— all combined to play their rolls in the drama.

Protesters displayed every sign slogan imaginable: No WTO! No Police State! No Government! F__K the Cops! Save the Whales! Free Tibet! and even the oddly and uncharacteristically humorous, Free Beer!

Businesses were trashed, concussion grenades exploded, rubber bullets zipped in every direction like a swarm of stinging hornets, and squads of riot-helmeted, baton- and pepper-spray-wielding officers responded to emergency after emergency after emergency— in Seattle?

Rioters set Dumpsters ablaze; anarchists hurled bottles of urine, flung bricks at officers, and fired steel ball bearings with wrist-rockets (slingshots); and officers jabbed protesters and noncompliant bystanders alike with long batons when multiple orders to disperse were ignored. One high-ranking police official was struck in the eye by a projectile and suffered serious injury.

One element of an event such as the WTO riots is, of course, in its sheer size; while many folks had similar experiences, dispersed by police with pepper spray and batons, perspectives differed depending on one's specific location and role in the melee. Probably the most sympathy should go to the media, for the many professional folks simply there to tell a story or record images, who got swept up in police efforts to clear rioters from the streets. Unfortunately, an order for everyone *except the media* to clear the streets would obviously be less than effective, and would likely have resulted in a sudden influx of folks with "media" credentials within the crowd.

It's clear that the many parties underestimated the evil intent of those relatively few who came to Seattle to specifically cause trouble. Many people proffered the idea that the police simply donning riot gear "fosters" violence. However, it's clear from any video of the incident that some folks came to legally make their voices heard, and some came to peacefully, through civil disobedience, impede the delegates from conducting their lawful business, while others came to illegally stop the WTO Conference from conducting any business at all—through violent means.

Many of these violent few, a significant number of whom had specifically learned to disrupt the event at training camps, moved as small squads through the crowd, concealing their faces with bandanas, hoods, and gas masks, creating hit-and-run havoc at commercial target after target, Starbucks, Nike, etc. These folks came prepared with a strategic battle plan and well-thought-out tactics, and they were armed with cell phones and weapons concealed within backpacks.

Other "legitimate" protest groups, city leaders, and some in the police command underestimated the relatively few but volatile demonstrators, accounting for much of the violence that occurred. The lessons learned by Seattle leaders and event organizers were many, but the most important was understanding that while planning for the best is fine, being prepared for the worst is essential.

# ALL SHOOK UP

2001

Chai, a nursing Indian elephant residing at the Woodland Park Zoo, suddenly bolted upright, raised her trunk high, and trumpeted in a manner unlike anything her keepers had ever seen in what, after the fact, could only be described as a warning of some mysterious and imminent event. Chai's four-month-old baby trumpeted as well, scooting to safety beneath her massive mother. Befuddled handlers recoiled at the pachyderm's unusual antics.

At the same moment in another part of the zoo, gorillas, shrieking like no keeper had ever seen, tore off in a panicked dash to the safety of their shelters. A frightened orangutan troop, apparently similarly affected, raced screeching to the trees and scrambled up to precarious perches among the highest branches, clinging on for dear life. In the days following the Nisqually earthquake, folks reported farm animals and domestic pets behaving much like those wild beasts residing in the zoo, apparently having sensed a rumble deep within the earth, which most humans apparently missed.

On the other hand, the two-legged primates known as *Homo sapiens* had little, if any, notice and most were taken completely by surprise when on February 27, 2001, a 6.8 magnitude earthquake rocked Seattle like none other since a 1949 quake at 7.1 magnitude wrecked significant property and killed eight people. A much-remembered earthquake that struck Seattle in 1965 was lower in Richter scale magnitude, but because it wasn't as deep within the earth as the 2001 quake, it had caused more damage than the Nisqually quake and killed seven people.

Over two hundred injuries, one death, and one to three billion dollars in damage occurred in the region. The city was already recoiling from a human quake that had rocked Seattle's Pioneer Square neighborhood the previous night. Rioters wreaked havoc at the annual Mardi Gras celebration, which was punctuated by the murder of a young man who'd come to the aid of a young woman who was being attacked by rioters. The earthquake not only shook the city but also knocked this tragedy off the front pages and snatched away TV news headlines.

Ironically, as if Bacchus himself was displeased with the corruption of the normally peaceful Mardi Gras festivities, most of the damage that occurred in Seattle was in the Pioneer Square area. The earthquake had knocked loose several historic building facades, sending brick, mortar, and concrete crashing onto the cars parked below. A good number of cars sustained minor to severe damage; as if a giant had stomped by, the debris literally flattened two cars to a height not reaching the average person's knee.

It is unbelievable that no pedestrians were injured by the many missiles that had rained down onto the pavement. In fact, the only death attributed to the earthquake was one woman who suffered a heart attack. Her death was reportedly partially due to her husband having been unable to make a timely 911 call due to phone lines jammed by frantic people.

Much of the damage was regional; the capitol building and other structures on the state government grounds in Olympia suffered significant damage. However, being the largest city, Seattle suffered a great deal of structural damage to its buildings and infrastructure. City and state officials also had to be aware of any potential damage to heavily used roadways, bridges, and other public facilities in the city. Much of Seattle's post-earthquake response involved surveying these structures for new cracks and any other loss of integrity.

A building that suffered significant damage was one of the oldest in the city. The venerable SODO (Sears & Roebuck's) building, erected in 1913 and now serving as Starbucks headquarters, was especially shaken by the quake. This building was once the largest building in the world by volume and is constructed upon tidal mud flats, which had been filled in by the dirt removed during the flattening of Denny Hill, a project much better known as the Denny Regrade.

Witnesses report employees dashing for doors and scrambling underneath desks as debris flew off shelves and was strewn throughout the offices. Much of the infrastructure of the building was compromised, including utilities such as the plumbing. The damage wasn't limited to the building's interior; a large chunk of the brick facade came crashing down around the perimeter of the building. Again, as in Pioneer Square a few blocks to the north, no one outside was injured.

A common description of the Nisqually earthquake was of a "rolling" effect it had on the land. Witnesses standing on sidewalks commented on the surreal scene of roadways undulating like black ribbons in a windstorm. Trees and utility poles swayed to and fro, and wires tugged taut and snapped slack as if a giant were playing with a toy town set. Cars stopped in place, and people on the streets responded in a variety of ways. Some dashed for doorway, some darted into the middle of the street, and others froze in place—petrified of whatever their imaginations conjured at such a moment.

Once the shaking had subsided, folks remained still, but a soothing sense of calm appeared to have descended on everyone as they began to realize they were going to survive the quake. However, people remained tense, perhaps concerned about any possible aftershocks. Later, they would learn that the epicenter of the quake was located near the Nisqually Indian Reservation, about thirty miles beneath their feet. Folks at the reservation reported some power outages, but like elsewhere, fortunately, no people were injured.

Although there was a considerable financial toll and some significant damage, scientists who study such things note that this seismological event was not the "Big One" that folks in the Pacific Northwest have been told about for years. In fact, in this case the quake occurred when the Juan de Fuca and North American tectonic plates collided, with the former sliding under the latter. This was the same cause as in the 1949 quake. However, scientists warn of the "Seattle Fault," which runs directly, and perilously, beneath the city's core. Scientists studying Seattle's ancient natural history believe it was along this fault line that a devastating earthquake ripped the landscape around the year A.D. 900.

Little apparent evidence remains from the Nisqually quake, most of the visible damage having been repaired. However, people might best remember that if they ever notice the lions, and tigers, and bears (oh, my!) become inexplicably agitated, or if Fido darts under the furniture or Tabby is suddenly clinging to the ceiling, they might want to take the hint and duck for cover—it might be the Big One.

# SEATTLE FACTS AND TRIVIA

- The first Birkenstock store in the United States was located in the Pike Place Market (MJ Feet).

- Technically Seattle's original name was Duwamps, but Seattle's founders called their temporary settlement New York, located at today's Alki.

- Seattle raised downtown street levels after the fire of 1889, in part to keep the toilets from backing up during high tide.

- Woodland Park was once a private estate that belonged to Anglophile Guy Phinney.

- Seattleites use this mnemonic device to help newcomers remember downtown streets: Jesus Christ Made Seattle Under Protest for (Jefferson/James), (Cherry/Columbia), (Marion/Madison), (Spring/Seneca), (University/Union), and (Pike/Pine).

- Vaudeville favorite Gypsy Rose Lee was born in Seattle in 1914.

- Robert Ripley, of *Ripley's Believe it or Not,* once called Seattle's Ye Olde Curiosity Shop "the greatest shop I ever got into."

- Bruce Lee's wife, Linda, was once Garfield High School's Homecoming Queen.

- Seattle's first television broadcast was of a high school football game.

- In 1997 *Almost Live* TV show host John Keister landed in hot water over his April Fool's Day joke, reporting that the Space Needle had fallen over, sparking freaked-out phone calls.

- Rock legends The Beatles and Led Zeppelin are among the stars that stayed at the famed Edgewater Inn when performing in Seattle.

- Seattle has America's largest movie-going population per capita.

- Seattle pioneer Asa Mercer was the inspiration for the character Jason Bolt, played by Robert Brown, on the *Here Come the Brides* TV series.

- *It Happened at the World's Fair,* starring Elvis Presley, was set at Seattle's 1962 World's Fair.

- Perry Como recorded "Seattle" as the theme song for the TV show *Here Come the Brides.*

- Ride the Ducks tour business uses vintage WWII amphibian landing craft offering a driving/sailing tour of Seattle.

- The 1992 film *Singles,* starring Matt Dillon and Bridget Fonda and featuring members of the bands Pearl Jam, Soundgarden, and Mudhoney, was filmed in Seattle.

- The 1974 John Wayne movie *McQ,* filmed in Seattle, included Seattle police officers as extras.

- Bruce Lee and his son, rising film star Brandon Lee, are laid to rest side by side in Lakeview Cemetery.

- Seattle became the first major American city to elect a woman to its highest office when Mayor Bertha Landes took office in 1926.

- The very first gas station was opened in Seattle in 1907, on East Marginal Way, and worked by a hand-cranked pump.

- Northgate Mall was the world's first covered shopping mall.

- In 1880, six feet of snow fell in Seattle between January 5 and 9.

- U.S. Customs agents once searched Winston Churchill upon his arrival in Seattle.

- The Seattle Police Department became the first modern department to deploy a bicycle patrol.

- The cost to build the Seattle Monorail: $3.5 million.

- An estimated half of the reported $200 million in gold from the 1896 Klondike Gold Rush remained in Seattle.

- Some work of Seattle cartoonist Gary Larson is displayed in the Smithsonian Institution.

- Mark Twain once said, "The nicest winter I ever spent was a summer in Seattle."

- On August 31, 1990, the Griffeys—Ken Jr. and Sr.—were the first father-son combo in major league history to play as teammates.

- Seattleite Bert Salisbury coined the sports term *windsurfing*.

- The Bumbershoot Festival is named for another word for umbrella.

- Seattleite Cheryl Linn Glass was the first black woman to become a professional race car driver.

- Seattle boasts seventy-two miles of maintained recreational trails and nine beaches.

- Seattle has thirty public libraries and seventeen museums.

- In Seattle you'll find sixty-one public parks, twenty-eight community centers, and five golf courses.

- Seattle has the most educated population in the United States with 91.9 percent having received a high school diploma, bachelor's degree, or higher.

- The Seattle area offers over nine thousand restaurants for your dining pleasure.

- Seattle's downtown business district has 11,890 hotel rooms.

- Seattle's top international trading partner is China.

- Seattle has twenty-one sister cities around the globe.

- Seattle is the northernmost U.S. city with a population of more than half a million.

- Of the 53,718 acres that make up Seattle, 6,189, or about 11.5 percent of those acres, are used for public parks.

- Seattle chartered the second chapter (after Oakland, California) of the Black Panther Party, founded in 1968.

- The giant online corporation Amazon.com is based in Seattle.

# BIBLIOGRAPHY

**Look What We Founded (1851)**

Andrews, Mildred Tanner. *Pioneer Square: Seattle's Oldest Neighborhood.* Seattle: University of Washington Press, 2005.

Bell, W. N. "William Bell: Pioneer Recollections, 1878." HistoryLink.org Essay 2653, 1878. www.historylink.org/index .cfm?DisplayPage=output.cfm&file_id=2653.

Crowley, Walt. "Denny, David Thomas (1832–1903)." HistoryLink.org Essay 1729, August 1998. www.historylink.org/ index.cfm?DisplayPage=output.cfm&file_id=1729.

———. "Denny Party scouts arrive at mouth of Duwamish River in future King County on September 25, 1851." Historylink .org Essay 5391, March 2003. www.historylink.org/index .cfm?DisplayPage=output.cfm&file_id=5391.

———. "John Low and Lee Terry select claims at Alki Point on September 28, 1851." Historylink.org Essay 1752, October 1999. www.historylink.org/index.cfm?DisplayPage=output .cfm&file_id=1752.

———. "Seattle—A Brief History of Its Founding." HistoryLink .org Essay 303, August 1998. www.historylink.org/index .cfm?DisplayPage=output.cfm&file_id=303.

Denny, Arthur Armstrong. *Pioneer Days on Puget Sound.* Fairfield: Ye Galleon Press, 1979.

Lange, Greg. "Collins party encounters Denny party scouts at
  Duwamish Head near future site of Seattle on September 27,
  1851." Historylink.org Essay 2765, November 2000. www
  .historylink.org/index.cfm?DisplayPage=output.cfm&file
  _id=2765.

———. "Denny party lands at Alki Point near future Seattle on
  November 13, 1851." HistoryLink.org Essay 5392, March
  2003. www.historylink.org/index.cfm?DisplayPage=output.cfm
  &file_id=5392.

———. "First contingent of Denny party relocates to site of
  Seattle on April 3, 1852." HistoryLink.org Essay 1956, January
  2000. www.historylink.org/index.cfm?DisplayPage=output.cfm
  &file_id=1956.

———. "Seattle and King County's First White Settlers."
  HistoryLink.org Essay 1660, October 2000. www.historylink
  .org/index.cfm?DisplayPage=output.cfm&file_id=1660.

Nordstrand, Dorothea. "Denny Party on the Oregon Trail."
  Historylink.org Essay 5647, February 2004. www.historylink
  .org/index.cfm?DisplayPage=output.cfm&file_id=5647.

———. "Pioneer Women of Seattle." HistoryLink
  .org Essay 7540, December 2005. www.historylink.org/index
  .cfm?DisplayPage=output.cfm&file_id=7540.

———. "Seattle's First Christmas." HistoryLink.org Essay 4138,
  January 2003. www.historylink.org/index.cfm?DisplayPage=
  output.cfm&file_id=4138.

Rochester, Janius. "Denny, Arthur Armstrong (1822–1899)."
  HistoryLink.org Essay 921, October 1998. www.historylink.org/
  index.cfm?DisplayPage=output.cfm&file_id=921.

Speidel, William C. *Sons of the Profits.* Seattle: Nettle Creek
  Publishing Company, 1967.

Stein, Alan J. "Seattle celebrates its 54th birthday and dedicates the Alki Point monument on November 13, 1905." HistoryLink .org Essay 3917, August 2002. www.historylink.org/index.cfm ?DisplayPage=output.cfm&file_id=3917.

Warren, James R. *King County and its Queen City: Seattle.* Woodland Hills: Windsor Publications Inc., 1981.

**General Sources:**

www.seattle.gov/

**The First Battle of Seattle (1856)**

Andrews, Mildred Tanner. *Pioneer Square: Seattle's Oldest Neighborhood.* Seattle: University of Washington Press, 2005.

Crowely, Walt, and David Wilma. "Native Americans attack Seattle on January 26, 1856." HistoryLink.org Essay 5208, February 2003. www.historylink.org/index.cfm?DisplayPage =output.cfm&file_id=5208.

Denny, Arthur Armstrong. *Pioneer Days on Puget Sound.* Fairfield: Ye Galleon Press, 1979.

Morgan, Murray. *Skid Road.* Seattle: University of Washington Press, 1951.

Phelps, T. S. "Reminiscences of Seattle, Washington Territory and the U. S. Sloop-of-War *Decatur* During the Indian War of 1855–56." *The United Service: A Monthly Review of Military and Naval Affairs 5 December 1881*, July 19, 2006. www.history .navy.mil/library/online/decatur_sloop.htm.

Speidel, William C. *Sons of the Profits.* Seattle: Nettle Creek Publishing Company, 1967.

Warren, James R. *King County and its Queen City: Seattle.* Woodland Hills: Windsor Publications Inc., 1981.

———. *Seattle: 150 Years of Progress.* Carlsbad: Heritage Media Group, 2001.

## Here Come the Brides (1864)

Andrews, Mildred Tanner. *Pioneer Square: Seattle's Oldest Neighborhood.* Seattle: University of Washington Press, 2005.

Lange, Greg. "Mercer Girls reach Seattle on May 16, 1864." HistoryLink.org Essay 166, November 1998. www.historylink .org/index.cfm?DisplayPage=output.cfm&file_id=166.

Morgan, Murray. *Skid Road.* Seattle: University of Washington Press, 1951.

Muhich, Peri. "Mercer Girls." HistoryLink.org Essay 1125, May 1999. historylink.org/index.cfm?DisplayPage=output.cfm&file _id=1125.

Speidel, William C., *Sons of the Profits.* Seattle: Nettle Creek Publishing Company, 1967.

Stein, Alan J. "*Here Come the Brides* debuts on ABC on September 25, 1968." HistoryLink.org Essay 1563, January 1999. www .historylink.org/index.cfm?DisplayPage=output.cfm&file_id =1563.

Warren, James R. *King County and its Queen City: Seattle.* Woodland Hills: Windsor Publications Inc., 1981.

———. *Seattle: 150 Years of Progress.* Carlsbad: Heritage Media Group, 2001.

## Remove Yourselves from the Northwest (1886)

Andrews, Mildred Tanner. *Pioneer Square: Seattle's Oldest Neighborhood.* Seattle: University of Washington Press, 2005.

"Anti-Chinese Riot at Seattle." *Harper's Weekly*, 6 March 1886. immigrants.harpweek.com/ChineseAmericans/Items/Item 095L.htm.

Hildebrand, Lorrain Barker. *Straw Hats, Sandals and Steel: The Chinese in Washington State.* Tacoma: The Washington State American Revolution Bicentennial Commission, 1977.

Lee, Jennifer. "Anti-Chinese Riots in Washington State." Dartmouth.edu, 2001. www.dartmouth.edu/~hist32/History/S01%20-%20Wash%20State%20riots.htm.

Morgan, Murray. *Skid Road.* Seattle: University of Washington Press, 1951.

PI. "Seattle mob rounds up Chinese residents and immigrant workers on February 7, 1886." HistoryLink.org Essay 2745, January 1900. www.historylink.org/index.cfm?DisplayPage=output.cfm&file_id=2745.

Warren, James R. *King County and its Queen City: Seattle.* Woodland Hills: Windsor Publications Inc., 1981.

———. *Seattle: 150 Years of Progress.* Carlsbad: Heritage Media Group, 2001.

Wei, William. "The Chinese-American Experience 1857–1892: The Anti-Chinese Hysteria of 1885–1886." HarpWeek.com. http://immigrants.harpweek.com/ChineseAmericans/2KeyIssues/TheAntiChineseHysteria.htm.

**Blazing Seattle (1889)**

Andrews, Mildred Tanner. *Pioneer Square: Seattle's Oldest Neighborhood.* Seattle: University of Washington Press, 2005.

Crowley, Walt. "Seattle burns down in the Great Fire on June 6, 1889." HistoryLink.org Essay 5115, January 2003. www.historylink.org/index.cfm?DisplayPage=output.cfm&file_id=5115.

Dorpat, Paul. "Now & Then—Seattle's Great Fire of 1889." HistoryLink.org Essay 2583, January 1999. www.historylink.org/index.cfm?DisplayPage=output.cfm&file_id=2583.

Morgan, Murray. *Skid Road*. Seattle: University of Washington Press, 1951.

Speidel, William C. *Sons of the Profits*. Seattle: Nettle Creek Publishing Company, 1967.

Warren, James R. *King County and its Queen City: Seattle*. Woodland Hills: Windsor Publications Inc., 1981.

———. *Seattle: 150 Years of Progress*. Carlsbad: Heritage Media Group, 2001.

## Down Under—Seattle (1889)

Andrews, Mildred Tanner. *Pioneer Square: Seattle's Oldest Neighborhood*. Seattle: University of Washington Press, 2005.

"Bill Speidel's Underground Tour." www.undergroundtour.com/ (accessed January 2009).

Crowley, Walt. "Underground tours of Pioneer Square begin in August 1964." HistoryLink.org Essay 3086, March 2001. www.historylink.org/index.cfm?DisplayPage=output.cfm&file_id=3086.

Speidel, William C. *Sons of the Profits*. Seattle: Nettle Creek Publishing Company, 1967.

———. *Through the Eye of the Needle*. Seattle: Nettle Creek Publishing, 1989.

## Thar's Gold in Them Thar Hills (1896)

Andrews, Mildred Tanner. *Pioneer Square: Seattle's Oldest Neighborhood*. Seattle: University of Washington Press, 2005.

Lange, Greg. "Klondike Gold Rush." HistoryLink.org Essay 687, January 1999. www.historylink.org/index.cfm?DisplayPage =output.cfm&file_id=687.

————. "Klondike Gold Rush begins on July 17, 1897." HistoryLink.org Essay 699, January 1999. www.historylink.org/ index.cfm?DisplayPage=output.cfm&file_id=699.

Morgan, Murray. *Skid Road.* Seattle: University of Washington Press, 1951.

Speidel, William C. *Sons of the Profits.* Seattle: Nettle Creek Publishing Company, 1967.

Stein, Alan J. "Seattle celebrates silver anniversary of Klondike Gold Rush on July 17, 1922." HistoryLink.org Essay 4311, July 2004. www.historylink.org/index.cfm?DisplayPage=output.cfm &file_id=4311.

Warren, James R. *King County and its Queen City: Seattle.* Woodland Hills: Windsor Publications Inc., 1981.

————. *Seattle: 150 Years of Progress.* Carlsbad: Heritage Media Group, 2001.

Wilma, David. "Gold prospectors travel north by the hundreds through Puget Sound to Alaska and the Yukon beginning in April 1895." HistoryLink.org Essay 8151, May 2007. www .historylink.org/index.cfm?DisplayPage=output.cfm&file_id =8151.

## They Moved Mountains (1898)

Crowley, Walt. "Seattle Neighborhoods: Belltown-Denny Regrade—Thumbnail History." HistoryLink.org Essay 1123, May 1999. www.historylink.org/index.cfm?DisplayPage =output.cfm&file_id=1123.

"Denny Regrade: Hosing Seattle into shape." *Seattle Daily Journal of Commerce,* December 1999. www.djc.com/special/century /10060862.htm.

Dorpat, Paul. "Seattle's Denny/Washington Hotel." HistoryLink .org Essay 2990, February 2001. www.historylink.org/index.cfm ?DisplayPage=output.cfm&file_id=2990.

Lange, Greg. "Denny Regrade contract for second phase is issued August 29, 1903." HistoryLink.org Essay 709, January 1999. www.historylink.org/index.cfm?DisplayPage=output.cfm&file _id=709.

―――. "Denny Regrade first phase is completed on January 6, 1899." HistoryLink.org Essay 708, January 1999. www.history link.org/index.cfm?DisplayPage=output.cfm&file_id=708.

―――. "Denny Regrade is completed after 32 years on December 10, 1930." HistoryLink.org Essay 711, January 1999. www .historylink.org/index.cfm?DisplayPage=output.cfm&file _id=711.

―――. "Denny Regrade second phase is completed on October 31, 1911." HistoryLink.org Essay 710, January 1999. www .historylink.org/index.cfm?DisplayPage=output.cfm&file _id=710.

Morgan, Murray. *Skid Road.* Seattle: University of Washington Press, 1951.

Seattle, Washington, Engineering Dept. "Guide to the Seattle Engineering Department Denny Hill Regrade Photograph Album 1904–1929." NWDA, 2004. http://nwdadb.wsulibs .wsu.edu/findaid/ark:/80444/xv95087.

Warren, James R. *King County and its Queen City: Seattle.* Woodland Hills: Windsor Publications Inc., 1981.

————. *Seattle: 150 Years of Progress.* Carlsbad: Heritage Media Group, 2001.

### A Walk in the Park (1903)

Historylink, and Friends of Olmsted Parks. "Olmsted Park Plans for Seattle Cybertour." HistoryLink.org Essay 7054, Sept. 2004. www.historylink.org/index.cfm?DisplayPage=output.cfm&file _id=7054.

"Park History-Olmsted Parks." Seattle Parks and Recreation Dept. www.seattle.gov/parks/parkspaces/olmsted.htm (accessed January 2009).

Warren, James R. *King County and its Queen City: Seattle.* Woodland Hills: Windsor Publications Inc., 1981.

Williams, David, and Walt Crowley. "John Olmsted arrives in Seattle to design city parks on April 30, 1903." HistoryLink .org Essay 3290, May 2001. www.historylink.org/index .cfm?DisplayPage=output.cfm&file_id=3290.

### In the Market for a Market (1907)

Andrews, Mildred Tanner. *Pioneer Square: Seattle's Oldest Neighborhood.* Seattle: University of Washington Press, 2005.

HistoryLink. "Pike Place Market Cybertour." HistoryLink.org Essay 7053 (2001). www.historylink.org/index.cfm?DisplayPage =output.cfm&file_id=7053.

Lange, Greg. "Seattle's Pike Place Market opens on August 17, 1907." HistoryLink.org Essay 1949, January 1999. www.history link.org/index.cfm?DisplayPage=output.cfm&file_id=1949.

Pike Place Market. "Pike Place Market Preservation & Development Authority (PDA)." www.pikeplacemarket.org/ frameset.asp?flash=true (accessed January 2009).

Speidel, Bill. *Through the Eye of the Needle.* Seattle: Nettle Creek Publishing, 1989.

Warren, James R. *King County and its Queen City: Seattle.* Woodland Hills: Windsor Publications Inc., 1981.

**First in the West to Scrape the Sky (1914)**

Andrews, Mildred Tanner. *Pioneer Square: Seattle's Oldest Neighborhood.* Seattle: University of Washington Press, 2005.

Crowley, Walt. "Seattle Neighborhoods: Pioneer Square— Thumbnail History." HistoryLink.org Essay 3392, June 2001. www.historylink.org/index.cfm?DisplayPage=output.cfm&file _id=3392.

Dictionary. "Definition: Skyscraper." Answers.com. www.answers .com/Skyscraper+history?gwp=11&ver=2.4.0.651&method=3 (accessed January 2009).

Lange, Greg. "Seattle's Smith Tower building permit is issued on October 20, 1910." HistoryLink.org Essay 727, January 1999. www.historylink.org/index.cfm?DisplayPage=output.cfm&file _id=727.

———. "Seattle's Smith Tower, tallest building west of Ohio, is dedicated on July 4, 1914." HistoryLink.org Essay 5370, March 2003. www.historylink.org/index.cfm?DisplayPage=output .cfm&file_id=5370.

Pastier, John. "Smith Tower (Seattle)." HistoryLink.org Essay 4310, July 1, 2004. www.historylink.org/index.cfm?DisplayPage =output.cfm&file_id=4310.

Warren, James R. *King County and its Queen City: Seattle.* Woodland Hills: Windsor Publications Inc., 1981.

Wilma, David. "Ivar Haglund buys Seattle's Smith Tower on May 19, 1976." HistoryLink.org Essay 2508, June 2000. www.historylink .org/index.cfm?DisplayPage=output.cfm&file_id=2508.

## Let's Dig a Trench (1917)

Crowley, Walt. "Lake Washington Ship Canal." HistoryLink.org Essay 1444, July 1999. www.historylink.org/index.cfm?Display Page=output.cfm&file_id=1444.

———. "Turning Point 11: Borne on the 4th of July: The Saga of the Lake Washington Ship Canal." HistoryLink.org Essay 3425, Jul. 2001. www.historylink.org/index.cfm?DisplayPage=output .cfm&file_id=3425.

HistoryLink.org Staff. "Seattle's Lake Washington Ship Canal is completed on May 8, 1917." HistoryLink.org Essay 5374, March 2003. www.historylink.org/index.cfm?DisplayPage =output.cfm&file_id=5374.

Lange, Greg. "Lake Washington Ship Canal construction starts on September 1, 1911." HistoryLink.org Essay 684, January 1999. www.historylink.org/index.cfm?DisplayPage=output.cfm&file _id=684.

Long, Priscilla. "Chinese laborers dig second Montlake Cut between Union Bay and Portage Bay in 1883." HistoryLink.org Essay 3349, June 2001. www.historylink.org/index.cfm ?DisplayPage=output.cfm&file_id=3349.

———. "Montlake log canal first connects Seattle's Union and Portage bays in 1861." HistoryLink.org Essay 3404, June 2001. www.historylink.org/index.cfm?DisplayPage=output.cfm &file_id=3404.

McRoberts, Patrick. "U.S.S. *Roosevelt*, in dedication ceremony, leads a marine parade through the Ballard locks on July 4, 1917." HistoryLink.org Essay 1422, June 1999. www.historylink.org/index.cfm?DisplayPage=output.cfm&file_id=1422.

Warren, James R. *King County and its Queen City: Seattle.* Woodland Hills: Windsor Publications Inc., 1981.

———. *Seattle: 150 Years of Progress.* Carlsbad: Heritage Media Group, 2001.

### The Wild Boeing Yonder (1917)

Andrews, Mildred Tanner. *Pioneer Square: Seattle's Oldest Neighborhood.* Seattle: University of Washington Press, 2005.

"Boeing." www.boeing.com (accessed January 2009).

Crowley, Walt. "William Boeing reportedly takes his first airplane ride on July 4, 1915." November 1998. http://historylink.org/index.cfm?DisplayPage=output.cfm&file_id=367.

Morgan, Murray. *Skid Road.* Seattle: University of Washington Press, 1951.

Speidel, Bill. *Through the Eye of the Needle.* Seattle: Nettle Creek Publishing, 1989.

Warren, James R. *King County and its Queen City: Seattle.* Woodland Hills: Windsor Publications Inc., 1981.

———. *Seattle: 150 Years of Progress.* Carlsbad: Heritage Media Group, 2001.

### Take This Job and . . . (1919)

Andrews, Mildred Tanner. *Pioneer Square: Seattle's Oldest Neighborhood.* Seattle: University of Washington Press, 2005.

Crowley, Walt. "Seattle—Thumbnail History." HistoryLink.org Essay 7934, September 2006. http://historylink.org/index .cfm?DisplayPage=output.cfm&file_id=7934.

Dorpat, Paul. "Now & Then—Seattle General Strike, 1919." HistoryLink.org Essay 2582, January 1999. http://historylink .org/index.cfm?DisplayPage=output.cfm&file_id=2582.

Morgan, Murray. *Skid Road.* Seattle: University of Washington Press, 1951.

Reider, Ross. "Seattle Union Record." HistoryLink.org Essay 2859, December 2000. www.historylink.org/index.cfm?DisplayPage =output.cfm&file_id=2859.

Warren, James R. *King County and its Queen City: Seattle.* Woodland Hills: Windsor Publications Inc., 1981.

———. *Seattle: 150 Years of Progress.* Carlsbad: Heritage Media Group, 2001.

## Cop Learns Bogus Booze Biz Busting Bootleggers (1925)

Andrews, Mildred. "Prohibition." HistoryLink.org Essay 405, December 1998. www.historylink.org/index.cfm?DisplayPage =output.cfm&file_id=405.

McClary, Daryl C. "Olmstead, Roy (1886–1966)—King of King County Bootleggers." Historylink.org Essay 4015, November 2002. www.historylink.org/index.cfm?DisplayPage=output.cfm &file_id=4015.

*Olmstead v. United States,* 277 U.S. 438, 48 S. Ct. 564, 72 L. Ed. 944 (1928). www.answers.com/topic/olmstead-v-united-states (accessed March 2009).

### Row, Row, Row Your Boat—Into History (1936)

Raley, Dan. "Events of the Century." *Seattle Post-Intelligencer* 21 December 1999, 12 January 2009. http://seattlepi.nwsource .com/sports/cent21.shtml.

Wahl, Grant. "Water World: The Evergreen State boasts an unmatched rowing tradition 100 years in the making." *Sports Illustrated,* November 17, 2003, January 12, 2009. http://sports illustrated.cnn.com/magazine/features/si50/states/washington/ water_world/.

### A Lynching at Fort Lawton (1944)

Denfeld, Duane Colt. "Fort Lawton to Discovery Park." Historylink.org, September 2008. www.historylink.org/index .cfm?DisplayPage=output.cfm&file_id=8772.

Moreno, Dominic W. *Riot at Fort Lawton, 1944.* Lincoln: iUniverse, Inc., 2004.

### Mysteries of the Deep (1942)

Crowley, Walt. "King County deeds Sand Point Airfield to U.S. Navy on February 1, 1921." Historylink.org Essay 365, November 1998. www.historylink.org/index.cfm?Display Page=output.cfm&file_id=365.

———. "U.S. Army flyers land at Sand Point Airfield to complete first aerial circumnavigation of the globe on September 28, 1924." Historylink.org Essay 364, November 2000. www .historylink.org/index.cfm?DisplayPage=output.cfm&file_id =364.

Lacitis, Erik. "Lake Washington's 'time machine' hooks divers." *Seattle Times.* http://community.seattletimes.nwsource.com/ archive/?date=20041129&slug=lakesecrets29m (accessed March 2009).

Lange, Greg. "King County transfers 413 Sand Point acres to the United States Navy on March 8, 1926." Historylink.org Essay 2303, May 2000. www.historylink.org/index.cfm?DisplayPage =output.cfm&file_id=2303.

———. "Lindbergh lands the *Spirit of St. Louis* in Seattle on September 13, 1927." Historylink.org Essay 877, February 1999. www.historylink.org/index.cfm?DisplayPage=output.cfm &file_id=877.

Submerged Cultural Resources Exploration Team. "Explorations Updates." Spring 2005. www.scret.org/Newsletters/2005Issue1 .pdf.

Wilma, David. "Military airplane lands at Sand Point for the first time on October 8, 1921." Historylink.org Essay 2242, January 2000. www.historylink.org/index.cfm?DisplayPage=output.cfm &file_id=2242.

## Seattle, Meet the World (1962)

Speidel, Bill. *Through the Eye of the Needle.* Seattle: Nettle Creek Publishing, 1989.

Stein, Alan J. "Century 21—The 1962 Seattle World's Fair, Part 1." Historylink.org Essay 2290, April 2000. www.historylink .org/index.cfm?DisplayPage=output.cfm&File_Id=229.

———. "Century 21—The 1962 Seattle World's Fair, Part 2." Historylink.org Essay 2291, April 2000. www.historylink.org/ index.cfm?DisplayPage=output.cfm&File_Id=229.

Warren, James R. *King County and its Queen City: Seattle.* Woodland Hills: Windsor Publications Inc., 1981.

# BIBLIOGRAPHY

## Java Men (1971)

Hoover's Profile: Starbucks Corporation. www.answers.com/starbucks
+history?afid=TBarLookup&nafid=27 (accessed March 2009).

Starbucks Coffee Company. www.starbucks.com/aboutus/overview
.asp (accessed March 2009).

Warren, James R. *Seattle: 150 Years of Progress.* Carlsbad: Heritage
Media Group, 2001.

## Murders Most Macabre (1983)

Crowley, Walt. "Three robbers raid Wah Mee gambling club in
the International District and kill 13 patrons on February 18,
1983." Historylink.org, February 2001. www.historylink.org/
index.cfm?DisplayPage=output.cfm&file_id=2984.

Johnson, Tracy. "Mak spared death for Wah Mee killings. Ruling
may finally settle 19-year legal fight." *Seattle Post-Intelligencer,*
April 30, 2002. http://seattlepi.nwsource.com/local/68438_mak
30.shtml.

Matthews, Todd. "Wah Mee Massacre." Historylink.org,
November 1998. www.historylink.org/index.cfm?DisplayPage
=output.cfm&file_id=382.

————. "Wah Mee, Seattle." Matthews, Todd, 1997. www
.wahmee.com/misc_wahmee.pdf (accessed January 2009).

Singer, Natalie. "23 years haven't erased grief cause by Wah Mee
Massacre." *Seattle Times,* September 2006. http://seattletimes
.nwsource.com/html/localnews/2003247239_wahmee07m.html
(accessed March 2009).

## Goodwill Running (1990)

"Goodwill Games Ceases Operations." www.goodwillgames.com/
(accessed March 2009).

"Past Goodwill Games. 1990 and Seattle." www.goodwillgames
.com/html/past_1990index.html (accessed March 2009).

Wilma, David. "Ted Turner's Goodwill Games open in Seattle on
July 20, 1990." Historylink.org Essay 5658, February 2004.
www.historylink.org/index.cfm?DisplayPage=output.cfm&file
_id=5658.

### The Incredible Sinking Bridge (1990)

Factbites.com. "Lacey V. Murrow Memorial Bridge." www.fact
bites.com/topics/Lacey-V.-Murrow-Memorial-Bridge (accessed
March 2009).

Higgins, Mark and Bailey, Gil. "Sections of Old I-90 Bridge Sink."
*Seattle Post-Intelligencer,* November 26, 1990. http://seattlepi
.nwsource.com/archives/1990/9011260018.asp.

NationMaster.com "The Lacey V. Murrow Memorial Bridge."
www.nationmaster.com/encyclopedia/Lacey-V.-Murrow
-Memorial-Bridge (accessed March 2009).

Stein, Alan J. "Lacey V. Murrow Memorial Bridge (Lake
Washington Floating Bridge) sinks on November 25, 1990."
Historylink.org Essay 2002, January 2000. www.historylink.org/
index.cfm?DisplayPage=output.cfm&file_id=2002.

### General Sources:

www.djc.com/news/ae/05003121.html.

www.findarticles.com/p/articles/mi_hb5249/is_199604/ai_n2004
5882.

www.gerwick.net/pdf/inland_waterways/033e_lacey_murrows.pdf.

www.wsdot.wa.gov/partners/irt/MaterialsSources/LVMBlueRibbon
PanelReport.pdf.

www.youtube.com/watch?v=gm0YQ3vuyyY.

# BIBLIOGRAPHY

## The Seattle Sound (1990)

Andrews, Mildred Tanner. *Pioneer Square: Seattle's Oldest Neighborhood.* Seattle: University of Washington Press, 2005.

Deming, Mark. "Mudhoney." *All Music Guide.* www.answers.com/topic/mudhoney-1 (accessed March 2009).

Hajari, Nisid. "Northwestern Exposure." *Entertainment Weekly,* March 1993. www.ew.com/ew/article/0,,30586,00.html (accessed March 2009).

Kerr, Dave. "Mudhoney—Endless Yesterdays." *The Skinny,* March 2006. www.theskinny.co.uk/article/39478-mudhoney-endless -yesterdays (accessed March 2009).

Prato, Greg. "Mark Arm." *All Music Guide.* www.answers.com/topic/mark-arm (accessed March 2009).

Silver Dragon Records. "The History of Grunge Music." www .silver-dragon-records.com/grunge.htm (accessed March 2009).

Sub Pop Records. http://subpop.com/about (accessed March 2009).

## The Day the Music Died—Again (1994)

NNDB. "Kurt Cobain." *Notable Names Database.* www.nndb.com/people/939/000025864/ (accessed March 2009).

Summers, Kim. "Kurt Cobain." *All Music Guide.* www.answers .com/topic/kurt-cobain (accessed March 2009).

## Four Heroes Gave Their All (1995)

Castro, Hector. "10 years ago, four perished in Pang warehouse blaze." *Seattle Post-Intelligencer,* January 5, 2005. http://seattlepi .nwsource.com/local/206590_pang05.html.

FEMA & USFA. "Four Firefighters Die in Seattle Warehouse Fire." *National Fire Data Center.* www.interfire.org/res_file/pdf/ Tr-077.pdf (accessed March 2009).

Nader, Eric & Wilson, Duff. "Fire Department Fined In Pang Blaze—Muzzling of Safety Chief Among 10 Violations Cited In Fatal Arson." *Seattle Times,* June 14, 2005. http://community .seattletimes.nwsource.com/archive/?date=19950614&slug =2126331.

Skolnik, Sam. "Pang's lawyer seeks to nullify prison term." *Seattle Post-Intelligencer,* February 17, 2005. http://seattlepi.nwsource .com/local/212429_pang17.html Feb 05.

Wallace, James, Dan Raley, & Ellis E. Conklin. "'Get the heck out of here!' Federal Team will probe cause of fire." *Seattle Post-Intelligencer,* January 7, 1995. http://seattlepi.nwsource.com/ archives/1995/9501080069.asp.

Wilma, David. "Four firefighters die in Pang arson fire in the International District on January 5, 1995." HistoryLink.org Essay 3820, May 2002. www.historylink.org/index.cfm?Display Page=output.cfm&file_id=3820.

### Bus Plunges off Bridge (1998)

Anderson, Rick. "The Silas File." *Seattle Weekly,* March 10, 1999. www.seattleweekly.com/1999-03-10/news/the-silas-file.php.

Hadley, Jane & Gordy Holt. "Some of the survivors will hurt a long time." *Seattle Post-Intelligencer,* December 1, 1998. http:// seattlepi.nwsource.com/archives/1998/9812020052.asp.

### The Second Battle of Seattle (1999)

Editorial. "Police and WTO Stamper takes the fall for other culprits." *Seattle Post-Intelligencer,* December 10, 1999. http:// seattlepi.nwsource.com/archives/1999/9912100127.asp.

Murphy, Kim. "Seattle Struggles to Regain Calm Following WTO Riots." *The Tech,* December 3, 1999; reprinted from *L.A. Times.* http://tech.mit.edu/V119/N63/seattle_wto.63w.html.

Postman, David. "Protesting Is Their Trade; World Trade Is Their Target—Campers Prepare For WTO Seattle Meeting—The WTO / The Globalize This! Action Camp." *Seattle Times,* September 20, 1999. http://community.seattletimes.nwsource .com/archive/?date=19990920&slug=2984244.

Postman, David, Jack Broom, & Warren King. "Clashes, Protests Wrack WTO—Police Try To Break Up Protesters; Clash Delays Opening Event." November 30, 1999. http:// community.seattletimes.nwsource.com/archive/?date =19991130&slug=2998492.

**General Sources:**

*Seattle PI.* http://seattlepi.nwsource.com/wto/.

*Seattle Times.* http://seattletimes.nwsource.com/special/wto/.

"WTO Activist Granted New Trial." http://archive.seattlepress online.com/article-9607.html.

**All Shook Up (2001)**

Crowley, Walt. "Earthquake registering 6.8 on Richter Scale jolts Seattle and Puget Sound on February 28, 2001." Historylink .org Essay 3039, March 2001. http://www.historylink.org/index .cfm?DisplayPage=output.cfm&file_id=3039.

Dizon, Kristin. "Remnants of Rattle in Seattle going, going, gone on eBay." *Seattle Post-Intelligencer,* March 20, 2001. http:// seattlepi.nwsource.com/lifestyle/quakesales20.shtml.

Johnson, Tracy. "10 years for 2001 Mardi Gras riot killing." *Seattle Post-Intelligencer,* February 28, 2006. http://seattlepi.nwsource .com/local/261101_thomas28.html.

Linn, Allison. "Bill Gates speech interrupted by quake." *Seattle Post-Intelligencer,* February 28, 2001. http://seattlepi.nwsource .com/business/gates28ww.shtml.

Staff. "Strong quake causes widespread damage in Northwest: Governor declares emergency in Western Washington." *Seattle Post-Intelligencer,* February 28, 2001. http://seattlepi.nwsource .com/local/quak28ww.shtml.

**General Sources:**

Kris Kime murder and Mardi Gras info. http://www.associated content.com/article/516923/the_ugly_side_of_mardi_gras.html ?cat=2.

The Nisqually Earthquake information clearinghouse. www.ce .washington.edu/~nisqually/index.html.

**Seattle Facts and Trivia:**

City of Seattle. Municipal Web site (accessed March 2009).

Hedtke, John V. *Washington Trivia.* Nashville: Rutledge Hill Press, 2001.

JCO. "World's First Gas Station." www.jetcityorange.com/Seattle/ Worlds-First-Gas-Station.html (accessed March 2009).

*National Geographic.* "World Wise Quiz: Seattle." http://travel .nationalgeographic.com/places/places-of-a-lifetime/seattle-quiz .html (accessed March 2009).

www.jetcityorange.com/Seattle/Seattle-trivia.html.

# INDEX

INDEX

## ABOUT THE AUTHOR

Steve Pomper is the author of *Is There a Problem Officer?* and *Seattle Curiosities*. He has been published in several magazines and webzines and writes a blog at www.stevepomper.com. Steve has served as a Seattle police officer for seventeen years. He lives, and plays, in the Great Pacific Northwest with Jody, his firefighter wife of thirty years.